Praise for

ROADMAP TO THE END OF DAYS

"Can cosmological time be aligned with biblical time? Is there a pattern leading up to the End of Days? In this epic undertaking, Friedmann cuts a clear path for the reader interested in life's biggest questions."
- **Jane Macdougall,** nationalpost.com/macdougall, @janemactweet

"Apocalyptists beware! The end of days is not upon us: not yet anyway. This book is full of fascinating facts, historical characters shown in a new light, and a peek at what lies ahead for all of creation."
- **Bernie Clark,** author of 'From the Gita to the Grail', and creator of www.YinYoga.com

"Friedmann has researched and composed another of his signature works deciphering the origins of the universe and decoding the unfolding apocalypse. With this seminal work, he achieves newfound heights, unraveling riddles of the past and piercing the veil that obscures future events. Stellar in the stature of his reflections, supreme in the depth of his details, he has gloriously composed a mesmerizing manuscript that leaves you spellbound."
- **David W. Menefee**, Pulitzer Nominated Author

"Daniel Friedmann's book, "Roadmap to the End of Days," is very insightful using the past and present narratives and sources in the Torah - Bible as a guide, the Universal Noahide Code (UNC), a means to bring about personal and global redemption to all people. As it says in the End of Days, the whole world will worship the one and only G-D may we see the Messianic Era today."
- **Rabbi Yakov D. Cohen,** television host of 'One People One World under G-D', and founder and director of the Institute of Noahide Code, a UN NGO, www.Noahide.org

Other Books by Daniel Friedmann

Inspired Studies Book 1: The Genesis One Code
Inspired Studies Book 2: The Broken Gift

The author's first book, *The Genesis One Code*, demonstrates an alignment between the dates of key events pertaining to the development of the universe and the appearance of life on Earth as described in Chapters 1 and 2 of Genesis, with those derived from scientific theory and observation.

The author's second book, *The Broken Gift*, follows and extends the scope of *The Genesis One Code* to include the appearance and early history of humans. Although the books stand alone and can be read in any order, reading them in the order of publication provides a comprehensive narrative starting with the beginning of the universe and proceeding until only a few thousand years ago.

So, we understand the past, but what about the present and future? Does the Bible also contain the timeline of human history and a timeline for the End of Days? Read the author's third book, *Roadmap to the End of Days,* and find out if you can place recent history in context and glimpse what is coming next.

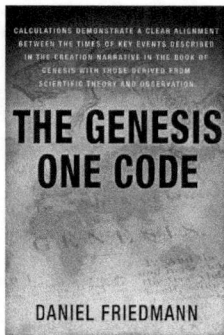

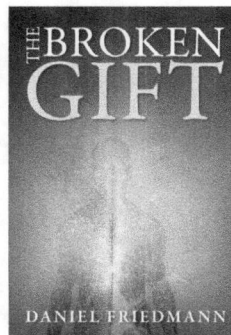

INSPIRED STUDIES

BOOK 3

Roadmap to the End of Days

Demystifying Biblical Eschatology to Explain the Past, the
Secret to the Apocalypse and the End of the World

Daniel Friedmann

Inspired Books

IB

Library and Archives Canada Cataloguing in Publication

Friedmann, Daniel E. (Daniel Eduardo), 1956-, author
Roadmap to the end of days: Demystifying Biblical Eschatology to explain the past, the secret to the apocalypse and the end of the world / Daniel Friedmann.

(Inspired Studies, Bk. 3)
Includes bibliographical references.
ISBN 978-0-9784572-3-5 (pbk.)

1. Eschatology. 2. Eschatology--Biblical teaching. I. Title.
II. Series: Friedmann, Daniel E. (Daniel Eduardo), 1956- . Inspired Studies, Bk. 3.

BT821.3.F75 2015   236   C2015-901192-2

ISBN: 978-0-9784572-3-5

10 9 8 7 6 5 4 3 2 1

DEDICATION

To Michael and Hugh, who are more interested in the end than in the beginning.

TABLE OF CONTENTS

FIGURES

TABLES

A Note from the Author

History is an academic discipline that uses a narrative to examine and analyze a sequence of past events and objectively postulate the patterns of cause and effect that determined them. Historians write in the context of their own time and with due regard to the current dominant ideas of how to interpret the past within the realm of natural causes. This book looks at history from the supernatural perspective.

The following joke, which I heard some time ago, illustrates the differences in approach:

> A little boy named Michael returned home from [Sunday] school and his father asked, "What did you learn today?"
>
> Michael answered, "Well, Dad, we learned how God sent Moses behind enemy lines on a rescue mission to lead his people out of Egypt."
>
> "How did he do that?"
>
> The boy said, "Moses was a strong wrestler and he beat Pharaoh up. Then while he was KO'd [knocked out], Moses got all the people together and ran towards the sea. When they got there, Moses had his engineers build a huge pontoon bridge and all the people walked across safely. Once they got to the other side, they blew up the pontoon bridge while the Egyptians were trying to cross."
>
> The father was shocked. "Is that really what the teacher taught you?"

The boy replied, "Well, no, Dad. But if I told you the story the way the teacher did, you'd never believe it!"[1]

We now embark on the true story of history.

Acknowledgments

Many people were instrumental in helping me with this work. My teachers of many years, Rabbi Avraham Feigelstock and Rabbi Shmuel Yeshayahu, introduced me to key concepts and helped me locate references.

Dania Sheldon provided extensive structural and copy editing, and Debra Christian and David W. Menefee provided critical editorial assistance. Alex Henning assisted with the design of all the tables and figures.

Karen Levitt, Paul Lim, Wendy Keizer, Jas Madhur, Suresh Jain, Andy Rechtshaffen, Dr. Joseph N. Trachtman, Hugh Boyle, Sol Pavony, Leticia Gomez, Richard Curtis, Karen Gantz, Justin Stone, Shelley Civkin and Gary Filippini provided valuable editorial comments, corrections and feedback.

I would also like to express my sincerest gratitude for the generous help and advice given to me by my wife, Marilyn, who patiently and repeatedly edited and formatted the manuscript.

Chapter 1

Introduction

Have you ever wandered around in a glass maze? The objective, of course, is to reach the exit. Along the way there are times when the exit seems just past the next glass pane, yet you turn and you are back in the middle of the maze, going around again. At times it feels like you are repeating the same section of the maze—or are you? After spending sufficient time stumbling along, you eventually reach the exit.

What about human history? Is it like a glass maze with a beginning and end—and some type of path(s) in between? Or is history a process with neither purpose nor direction? Does history repeat itself in some mindless or mindful sense?

If we could stand above the glass maze, we could clearly see its pattern, the way we traveled through it, the way we could have navigated through it to reach the exit sooner, or the path someone currently within the maze must follow to get out.

If history is like a glass maze, can we "stand above" it and observe the pattern? Can we see where we have been? Where and what historical events have repeated themselves—albeit not identically? Can we determine where we are right now, and what pattern has been unfolding before us? Can we find the future, the exit? Is there more than one way to get there?

Most religions see history as a maze. History has a beginning, depicted by a creation story culminating in the appearance of humans. History has an end, described by a time period known as the 'End of Days.' The Abrahamic faiths maintain a linear cosmology, with End of Days scenarios outlining themes of transformation and redemption.[1] The non-Abrahamic faiths maintain more cyclical views, with the final events in history characterized by decay, redemption, and rebirth. Nonetheless, within any cycle there is a beginning and an end, and the various descriptions of the end bear some similarities to those found in linear cosmologies. As to the period between the beginning and the end, there is less agreement among the different faiths; nonetheless, thousands of years of actual history may be studied for enlightenment. Through the ages, many groups have thought, at various times, that they were close to the End of Days—seemingly just one glass pane away from the exit of the maze—only to have history reveal there was still some time remaining!

The End of Days

What happens as we approach the exit of the maze, the end of history?[2]

The most famous description, that of universal peace, comes from the book of Isaiah:

> *And He shall judge among the nations, and shall rebuke many people: and they shall beat their swords into plowshares, and their spears into pruning hooks: nation shall not lift up sword against nation, neither shall they learn war any more.* [3]

Very appealing! As we search through the biblical texts, there are many more references to the End of Days and to the events leading up to this period. Some references are exciting, like universal peace once we get there, as described above; and unfortunately, some are very disheartening, like cataclysmic war while en route.

Some descriptions of events leading to the End of Days seem contradictory, and many are hard to understand. Interpretations vary as to how the End of Days will unfold, in what order the events will occur, and how to fit all the scriptural references together into a coherent picture.

One source of confusion comes from the fact that different faiths are based on dissimilar beliefs and interpretations. For example, the three largest Abrahamic religions (Judaism, Christianity, and Islam) believe the End of Days is a Messianic Age, a future time of universal peace and brotherhood on Earth, without crime, war, and poverty. This age is ushered in by a Messiah. However, the similarities stop there;[4] for example, Jewish and Christian views of the nature and identity of the Messiah diverge. Events in the End of Days also have similarities and differences. Within the Jewish and Christian traditions for instance, there is the notion of personal trials, tribulations, and even cataclysmic struggles prior to the redemption: *"And evil will befall you in the end of days."*[5]

The Jewish and Christian versions of the apocalypse are dissimilar: one difference being the concept of Satan.[6] In Judaism, Satan is an accusing angel—a sort of cosmic prosecuting attorney acting entirely under God's control—who condemns the people when they stray from their historic mission. In some Christian denominations, the notion of Satan is different and encompasses a dualistic perception of a powerful anti-God antagonist who battles the Almighty for the destiny of the human race.

Another source of confusion comes from the interpretation of scripture within a particular faith.[7] For example, some faiths hold the perspective that the scenario relating to the End of Days is more or less fixed, thus trying to fit all biblical references into that one scenario. This is analogous to a glass maze where only one path leads to the exit. But what if the maze has multiple paths leading to the exit?

Judaism teaches that all 'good' prophecy will eventually be fulfilled—in other words, universal peace will arrive.[8] When and how? That depends on our actions. We can either hasten or delay the Messianic Era, depending on how we behave. "Bad" prophecy, like apocalyptic war, is a warning. It can come true if that is required to help us follow God's laws, but it can also be avoided through proper action and behavior. Thus, when and how the Messianic Era will arrive depends on us. The maze offers several paths to the exit.

In this case, references to events in the End of Days relate to various scenarios and are not contradictory. Nonetheless, fitting these together in the differing scenarios is a matter of some disagreement. In addition, most believe that scenarios for the End of Days cannot be completely worked out, and what the scriptures mean will only be clear when we get there.

The Blueprint for History

If history is a controlled process from a beginning to an end—albeit with varied scenarios depending on our actions—where do we find more information on the process? There is one document that claims to be the blueprint for Creation: the Bible.[9]

Many Christians and Jews consider the Five Books of Moses to be the revealed Word of God. To some, this means the words contained in those books, along with other scriptures and the Oral Tradition that elaborates and explains the Five Books, were given to Moses in exactly the form we have them today.[10] To others, this means that God spoke to men—mainly prophets—who recorded His words in the book widely known as the Bible. Scholars estimate that the Bible was written by 40 people over a span of 2,000 years. And, to non-believers, the Bible is a collection of ancient myths and fables.

The Holy Bible, the sacred writings of the Christian religion, comprised of the Old Testament (containing 39 books of Hebrew scripture, including the Five Books of Moses) and the New Testament. The latter includes the four Gospel accounts of Jesus' life and teachings, as well as letters, mainly from the apostle Paul, written to encourage and inspire new church groups that sprang up in the wake of Jesus' ministry. The New Testament culminates in the Book of Revelation—the story of events leading up to the End of Days and the Messianic Age.

The Islamic holy book is the Qur'an. In addition, there are other revelations, which most Muslims believe were dictated by God to various Islamic prophets. These revelations include the Tawrat (given to Moses, and which is close[11] to the Five Books of Moses), the Zabur (revealed to David and is close to Psalms), and the Injil (teachings revealed through Jesus).

For Jews, the Written Law, in particular the Five Books of Moses, is interpreted and applied with the aid of the Oral Law (now documented in writing). The Oral Law includes the Talmud and the Zohar. The Talmud (meaning instruction or learning) is a central text of mainstream Judaism in the form of a record of rabbinic discussions pertaining to Jewish law, ethics, philosophy, customs, and history. The Zohar (meaning splendor or radiance) is the foundational work in the literature of Jewish mystical thought known as Kabbalah. Together, the Written and Oral Law comprise the Torah.[12]

Talmudic sages teach that *"God looked into the Torah and created the world."*[13] The Torah is the blueprint for the universe and humankind's existence from a faith-based perspective, and it is drawn from a tradition of oral and written principles.

The Torah describes an all-powerful God who acts purposefully, transforming history into a controlled process that leads to a specific destination. However, as explained earlier, humanity—based on its actions—alters the exact path and time taken to reach the destination.[14] Are we provided with information about different paths to the destination? Yes. Is there a default path to be followed if we do not behave properly? Maybe. Is there a guarantee that we will get to the End of Days, no matter what actions we take? Yes.[15] Is there a guaranteed maximum allowed time to get there? Yes.[16] Can we decipher some of these exact answers from the blueprint? Yes, we can when it comes to the maximum time allowed, and, as previously discussed, we have significant information about the possible paths.

What about the rest? Can we tell what will happen and when? Can we place history in perspective; can we see today's events as part of the process? Read on and decide.

First, we must understand the biblical chronology.

Time in the Bible, Science, and History

We take time for granted, yet it is an exceedingly difficult concept. Time is a dimension in which events can be ordered from the past through the present into the future, along with the measure of durations of events and the intervals between them. Time has long been a major subject of study in religion, philosophy, and science, but defining it in a manner applicable to all fields has consistently eluded scholars.

Scientists have established that time has a beginning, may have an end, and varies for people within different frames of reference.[17] The Big Bang theory leads to an initial singularity from which the universe and time emerged—the beginning of time. Some theories point to many scenarios within which time, and perhaps also the universe, end.[18] Einstein's theories of special relativity and general relativity, although counter-intuitive, show that people moving with respect to each other and/or in dissimilar gravitational fields experience time differently, and neither is absolute or universally correct. These theories have been tested and confirmed.

Similarly, time in the Bible has a beginning and an end, and it is different for the two separate observers of whom the Bible speaks: God and humans. Genesis sets out from a point *"in the beginning"* of time. The Scriptures tell us, as will be elaborated later in the book, that the world will attain a Messianic age and will eventually perhaps even cease to have a physical manifestation.[19] Finally, the Scriptures and their mystical interpretation reveal that time is kept differently in the physical world and in the various spiritual strata, or worlds.[20]

The biblical chronology consists of three stages or eras of time, as depicted in Figure 1.1: the 6 Days of Creation, followed by 6,000 years of history, followed by the 1,000 years of the seventh millennium.[21]

Biblical Calendar – Creation time						Biblical Calendar – Human history						7th millennium
Day 1	Day 2	Day 3	Day 4	Day 5	Day 6	1000	2000	3000	4000	5000	6000	7000
Corresponds to 13.74 billion years						Corresponds to 3760 BCE until 2240 CE						

Figure 1.1 The Three Stages of Biblical Chronology

The six Days of Creation can be shown to correspond to about 13.74 billion years and to depict the events and timeline for the formation of the universe, as well as the appearance of life on Earth and the prehistory of humans.[22] During this period, God is keeping time, so the "Creation days" must be converted to "time as kept by humans" with one Creation day being about 2.5 billion years.[23] The next 6,000 years correspond approximately to human history and match the Gregorian calendar from 3760 BCE to 2240 CE.[24] Scripture designates the Messianic Era, or End of Days, as starting on or before the year 6000 (2240 CE) and transitioning to the seventh millennium. During the seventh millennium, God once again will keep time, and these 1,000 years will correspond to a long period of time as experienced by us.[25]

The Biblical Timeline and the Origins of Israel

The Five Books of Moses contain not only the 6 Days of Creation but also a history of the first 2,500 or so years until the Israelites receive the Torah and are poised to enter Israel (1273 BCE).[26] Beyond that, other Bible texts, such as Kings, elaborate on later history—for instance the period of the First Temple (which was the first central sanctuary in Jerusalem to serve as the physical abode of the indwelling of God's Presence on Earth). In total, the Bible provides a narrated history that begins about 1500 BCE and extends to around 350 BCE, from Israel's remembered origins in its founding ancestors through to its emergence as a people and a kingdom. It continues by recording Israel's and then Judah's experiences of conquest and deportation at the hands of Assyria and then Babylonia, and finally to Israel's rebuilding as a nation during the Persian Empire. The Oral tradition then further extends the history through the time of the Second Temple and the compilation of the Oral tradition, well into the early Common Era. By piecing all the sources together, one can generate an exact biblical timeline that seamlessly merges into the general modern historical timeline and places all events—from Creation, through to the revelation at Sinai, until today.[27] A summary of the biblical timeline, showing the biblical and Gregorian calendar year for each event, can be found in Appendix A.

Throughout the Torah's historical account, the meaning of the word 'Israel' shifts over time from referring to a person (Jacob), to the 12 Tribes that descend from Jacob, to the nation that receives the revelation at Sinai, to a united monarchy, to a divided monarchy, and finally, to a people exiled,[28] for now about 2,000 years.

The story of Jacob wrestling with an angel is our first encounter with the word 'Israel' in the Bible (Genesis 32:24–32), where it clearly refers to a person. (The biblical chronology of Israel starts at 2205, or 1556 BCE.) Jacob had 12 sons, whose descendants became the 12 Tribes and then the nation of Israel in the books of Exodus, Joshua, and Judges (approximately 1570 to 900 BCE).

In the first book of Samuel, Israel is the name of a united monarchy headed by King David and his son Solomon. Here, Israel denotes a kingdom made up of 12 Tribes (approximately 880 to 800 BCE).

After only 75 years, the united monarchy is divided (see I–II Kings). A rebellion within the 12 Tribes results in a schism; Israel becomes the designation for the 10 northern tribes, and Judah becomes the designation for the southern territory occupied by the remaining two tribes, of Judah and Benjamin.[29] Israel during this time of the divided monarchy (approximately 800–550 BCE) is still a kingdom but smaller.

The northern kingdom of Israel falls to Assyria (approximately 556 BCE). Assyria's deportation policy is to disperse and divide the conquered people, which is how the 10 Tribes are 'lost.'[30]

The southern kingdom of Judah falls to Babylonia, and the First Temple is destroyed (approximately 423 BCE). Babylonia's deportation policy (carried out in several waves) is to keep the upper and middle classes together as one people and use their expertise and power; as such, Judah continues to exist in exile. In addition, a number of people from the northern kingdom (the 10 Tribes) move south soon after the division of the kingdoms (because they do not agree with the religious changes made by the northern king), and many others from the northern kingdom manage to escape south during the Assyrian conquest. Thus some of the members of the 10 Tribes survive with Judah. In addition, the lower class is not deported.[31]

On the return to the homeland (approximately 350 BCE, recounted in the books of Ezra and Nehemiah), the exiles from Babylonia complete the Second Temple. Ezra the scribe officially publishes the 24 books of the written Torah before his death in 313 BCE.

Then come periods of Greek and Roman influence and often domination, culminating with the destruction of the Second Temple (69 CE) and subsequent exile.[32] Throughout this period and later, the Oral Torah continues to be compiled, and the Talmud is completed in 475 CE.

Beyond the Torah historical account described above, we have other supporting evidence.[33] Archaeological studies of the land of ancient Israel and the surrounding ancient Near East have proven helpful in giving daily life and worship more color, often corroborating the biblical texts. Archaeological excavation has also yielded royal texts[34] that provide an outsider's view of Israel. These texts provide alternate versions of how certain events happened (e.g., a particular king retreated voluntarily as opposed to being beaten in battle), but often corroborate what happened and when (e.g., the king did exist at the time, did come to the area, but did not destroy the city).

The Concept of this Book

As this book will demonstrate, we have: a clear biblical timeline comprising thousands of years of human history; a chronology of actual history until today—the Jewish year 5777 or 2017 CE; a deadline for the End of Days—i.e., the year 6000 or 2240 CE; and numerous sources describing events relating to the End of Days.

In addition, we will learn about numerous sources describing historical events where we have been close to the End of Days but failed to get there, and sources that describe the metaphysical meaning of key historical events.

Finally, there are sources that claim the Torah foretells the course of human history in a number of ways. For example, the Ramban (a leading medieval scholar, rabbi, and biblical commentator who lived from 1194 to 1270 CE) says that the whole of human history is hinted at in the 6 Days of Creation.[35]

The premise of this book is that there is information in scripture and history: (i) to place history in context with the Divine Plan (i.e., God's plan for history and humanity); (ii) to realize where we are presently with respect to the End of Days; (iii) to grasp the default scenario in which the End of Days will come about (assuming we don't do the right things and bring it earlier and less painfully); (iv) to recognize the chain of events that will usher in the default scenario for the End of Days (both those events that have already happened and future events that are unfolding); and (v) to understand the approximate time frame within which the default scenario of these events will occur—i.e., not the exact time, but to within about 40 years.

The Organization of this Book

Past and future events, described and plotted on a timeline and superimposed on a plan for human history, will provide readers with the roadmap to the End of Days. The book will focus primarily on the high-level description of critical events and the corresponding timeline, with diagrams and tables. Details are provided in the Appendices, Endnotes (including all references), and Glossary of terms used and personalities mentioned in the main text. You may choose to ignore these, consult them while reading the book, or review them after a first reading of the main text.

Following this Introduction, which outlines the overall text, Chapter 2 summarizes the Cosmic Purpose of Creation, providing background for the understanding of historical events within the context of the Divine Plan.

In Chapter 3, the Messianic Era is described, outlining the scriptural background to help readers recognize key events and personalities.

In Chapter 4, the universal timeline and the specific pattern of relational history is developed.

Chapter 5 looks back at the almost 6,000 years of elapsed biblical history within the pattern developed in Chapter 4, where the specific pattern of history becomes evident.

In Chapter 6, we look at recent history (the 20th and early 21st centuries), comparing recent events with events from long ago and those described in the prophetic scriptures. Of course, hindsight is 20/20. Nonetheless, recent history will come into focus in an amazing and revealing way.

In Chapter 7, we are reminded of the disclaimer that comes with this work. History's interpretation is up to us, and future events are within our making. Although the end result and maximum time to attain it are guaranteed, it is up to us how and when we get to the End of Days. This book discusses a default scenario that may unfold if we do not take control of destiny.

In Chapter 8, we look forward. Having traced the cosmic placement of events, both historical and present, the pattern of the future becomes clear. The sequence of events and their approximate time as they relate to the End of Days will be obvious, as will their match to prophetic scripture.

In Chapter 9, we look beyond the End of Days and glimpse the life in the World to Come.

By the time we reach the conclusion in Chapter 10, the bird's-eye view of where we have been and where we might go will bring us to a new level of understanding and a further questioning of our human origins, purpose, destiny, and ability to alter the path to the future.

Chapter 2

The Cosmic Purpose and the Struggle to Achieve It

The Cosmic Purpose

Why are we here? What is life all about? What is the purpose of existence? A large number of answers to these questions have been proposed, from many different cultural and ideological backgrounds. The answers range from the view that each person is free and creates the meaning of his or her life, to the Abrahamic religions' view of God creating the world and working through history to reach the End of Days and fulfill His Cosmic Purpose.

What is this Cosmic Purpose?

> *The purpose for which this world was created is that the Holy One, blessed be He, desired to have an abode in the lower worlds.*[1]

"An abode in the lower worlds." What does that mean? The term 'world' in Hebrew, *olam*, actually means concealment. The concept is that during Creation, God withdrew or concealed himself so we could exist and exercise free will. The extent of the concealment was such that one can even doubt God's existence.

It is our task to reveal God's essence, "transforming the world's superficial obscurity into an environment in which God's Presence is felt, and in which He feels (so to speak) at home."[2]

How Do We Accomplish this Cosmic Purpose?

The Cosmic Purpose is achieved by humankind at large observing the Seven Noahide Laws[3] that provide any society with civilized foundations, and by Jews specifically observing the 613 commandments of the Torah.

At the heart of this universal moral code of laws is the acknowledgment that morality—indeed, civilization itself—must be predicated on the belief in God. Unless we recognize a higher power to whom we are responsible and who observes and knows our actions, we will not transcend the selfishness of our character and the subjectivity of our intellect. If each person is the final arbiter of right and wrong, then 'right' for him or her will be what he or she desires, regardless of its consequences for the other inhabitants of Earth.[4]

The Seven Noahide Laws are:[5]

1. The prohibition of idolatry:

    Acknowledge that there is only one God, who is Infinite and Supreme above all things. Do not replace that Supreme Being with finite idols, whether yourself or other beings. This command includes such acts as prayer, study, and meditation.

2. The prohibition of murder:

    Respect human life. Every human being is an entire world. To save a life is to save that entire world. To destroy a life is to destroy an entire world.[6] To help others live is a corollary of this principle.

3. The prohibition of theft:

    Respect the rights and property of others. Be honest in all your business dealings.

4. The prohibition of sexual immorality:

    > Respect the institution of marriage. Marriage is a most
    > Divine act. Disloyalty in marriage is forbidden.

5. The prohibition of blasphemy:

    > Respect God. As frustrated and angry as you may be,
    > do not vent it by cursing Him.

6. The prohibition of eating flesh taken from an animal while it
    is still alive:

    > Respect God's creatures. At first, Man was forbidden
    > to consume meat. After the Great Flood, he was
    > permitted to eat meat—but with a warning: do not
    > cause unnecessary suffering to any creature.

7. The requirement of maintaining courts to provide legal
    recourse.

    > Maintain justice. We are responsible for laying down
    > necessary laws and enforcing them whenever we can.
    > When we right the wrongs of society, we are acting as
    > partners in the act of sustaining the world.

Humanity failed to keep the Seven Noahide Laws. At Mount
Sinai, God charged the Children of Israel with the responsibility to
serve as His "*Light unto the nations*"[7] by bringing all of humanity to a
recognition of its Creator and an adherence to His laws.[8] To
accomplish this mission, the Israelites were provided with an
expanded set of laws: the 613 commandments[9] of the Torah. These
613 commandments, which include both the 10 Commandments
(more accurately translated as the 10 Sayings) and are also
encompassed by them,[10] are laws concerning every aspect of life—
for example: laws on how to conduct one's business and treat one's
employees; laws of marriage, divorce, and family; and laws relating to
forbidden sexual relations. Many commandments can be observed
today,[11] such as most of the examples listed above, keeping the

Sabbath, and eating kosher food.[12] However, many of these commandments cannot be observed today because they relate to observances associated with the Temple, its sacrifices, and its services (because the Temple does not exist), and with criminal procedures (because the theocratic state of Israel does not exist).[13]

Maimonides (the preeminent Jewish philosopher) states that Moses was commanded by God to compel the world to accept the Seven Noahide Laws. For many centuries, however, the circumstances did not allow this to be done. In 1983, Rabbi Menachem M. Schneerson said it was time to revitalize the observance of the Seven Noahide Laws. As a result, in 1987, President Ronald Reagan signed a proclamation regarding "the historical tradition of ethical values and principles, which have been the bedrock of society from the dawn of civilization when they were known as the Seven Noahide Laws, transmitted through God to Moses on Mount Sinai," and in 1991 the United States Congress did the same.[14]

The Seven Noahide Laws and the 613 commandments will be observed in the End of Days, or the Messianic Era, when all humankind will be sufficiently sensitized to perceive God. At that time, when all creatures will know their Creator, His dwelling place will be complete:

> and the Lord will reign forever and ever[15] and . . . the Lord will be king over the entire earth; on that day the Lord will be One and His Name One.[16]

The ultimate purpose of Creation is thus the Messianic Era and the period that follows it, and these will be achieved by observing God's laws.

Sounds reasonably easy, right? Apparently not! Right at the beginning, when there was only one commandment to obey, Adam failed to do so. Had he obeyed it for three more hours,[17] until the end of Day 6, the Cosmic Purpose would have been fulfilled.

However, in the wake of the sin of the Tree of Knowledge of Good and Evil, God's Divine Presence departed from the Garden of Eden. Later, on account of the sin of Cain and then of Enosh,[18] followed by the generation of the Flood, the Divine Presence withdrew even further from this world, and so on.[19] Then progress in the right direction restarted with Abraham and continued with other God-fearing people, until Moses, when the Divine Presence rested in the Tabernacle (a temporary, mobile sanctuary constructed by the Jewish people during their journey in the desert).[20] Later, the people's sin displaced the Divine Presence, but it was brought close again with the construction in Jerusalem of the First Temple and, eventually, the Second. People's persistent sinfulness, however, brought about the destruction of both Temples,[21] leaving unfinished the task of drawing down the Divine Presence. Finally, in the End of Days, the Third Temple will be built, and the Divine Presence will be revealed in the world.[22]

The sequence is straightforward: first comes Creation and prehistory, and then comes the (up to) 6,000-year period of history, in which the Divine Purpose of Creation plays out. Finally, at the end of history, after the End of Days, or the Messianic Era, when humanity as a whole completes its mission of making the physical world a dwelling place for God, will come the era of universal reward—the seventh millennium, or the Millennium, as its referred to by some Christian denominations.

So why is it so hard to get to the destination? What keeps getting in the way?

The Struggle

Two groups keep interfering with the Cosmic Purpose: humanity and Amalek. We have already seen that Adam tripped up by disobeying God's first command. During the times of the Temples, people sinned and therefore prevented the Cosmic Purpose from being achieved. Thus, the human animalistic drive[23] that leads to sin has been and continues to be the main obstacle.

The second obstacle is the nation of Amalek, whose purpose is to maintain the separation between the Divine and this world. Every time we are close to achieving the Cosmic Purpose, the nation of Amalek[24] attacks, suicidally at times, to disrupt the process of creating a dwelling place for the Divine on Earth. When Amalek attacks, even if it loses the battle and is badly decimated, it succeeds in dampening spiritually charged spirits, as it has done each time the Cosmic Purpose has been close at hand.

Amalek's Interference

Who is the nation of Amalek? Today we don't know—too much racial mixing has occurred to pinpoint it. But we do know its purpose. In Hebrew, *amalek* means doubt. Thus, the nation's purpose is to instill doubt and prevent us from achieving the Divine goal. The original Amalek was the grandson of Esau, one of the two sons of Isaac, who was a son of Abraham, see Figure 2.1 Abraham's Family.[25]

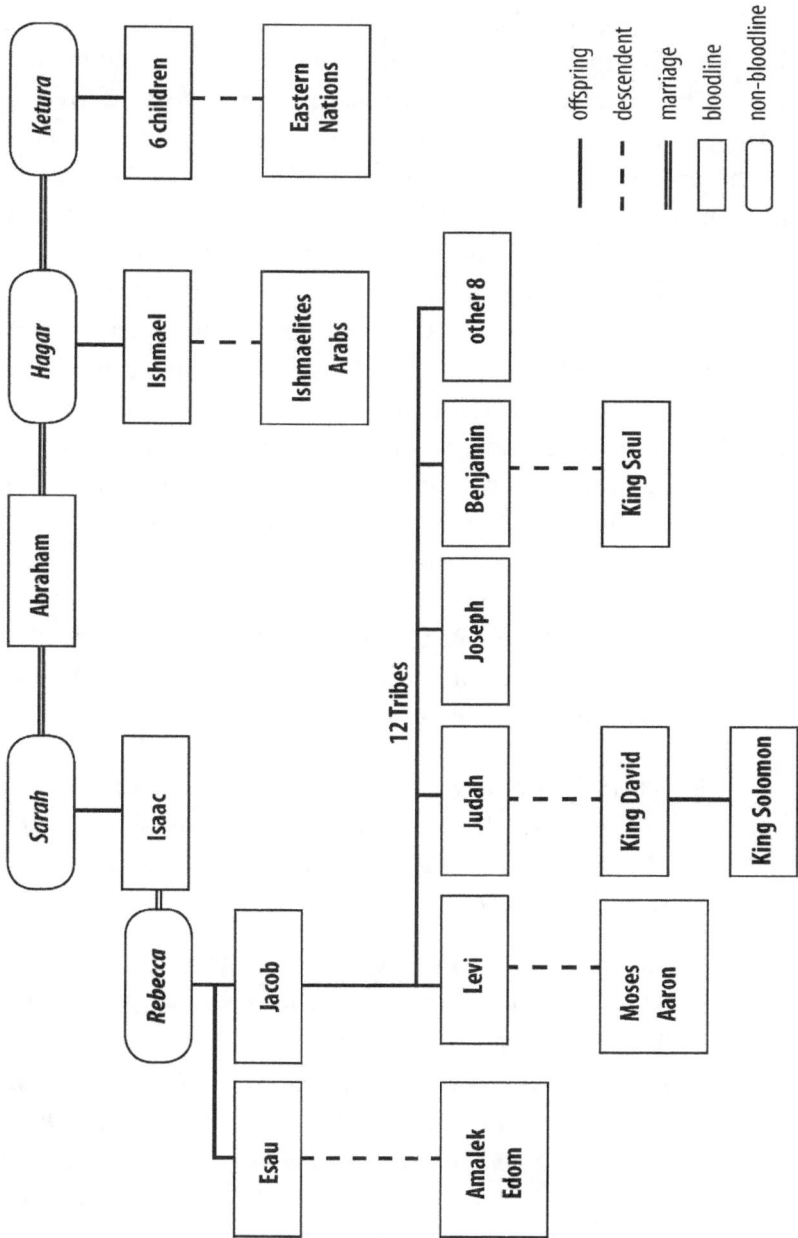

Figure 2.1 Abraham's Family

The other son of Isaac was Jacob. Jacob and Esau struggled before and after their birth as twins, representing an ongoing cosmic conflict. The struggle with Amalek is sometimes also referred to as the struggle with Edom, the name given to Esau's descendants.

The origin of this account actually goes back to Adam. He ate fruit from the Tree of Knowledge of Good and Evil, which is described in Kabbalah as the tree of doubt. Why? Because before that point, good, meaning closeness to the Creator, and evil, meaning a gap or separation from the Creator, were clear. After Adam ate, good and evil mixed, the clarity was lost, and doubt came into the world. Jacob and Esau represented these two critical concepts: closeness to and separation from the Creator. During Jacob's and Esau's lifetime, when Jacob was trying to establish the tribes of Israel, the brothers competed for rulership on Earth—closeness to the Creator, and therefore fulfillment of the Divine Purpose, or separation from the Creator.[26]

That same struggle re-emerged as Amalek attacked suicidally, but unsuccessfully, at the time of the Exodus, when Moses was leading the formation of the nation of Israel:[27]

> *Amalek came and attacked the Israelites at Rephidim. Moses said to Joshua, "Choose some of our men and go out to fight the Amalekites. Tomorrow I will stand on top of the hill with the staff of God in my hand."*

> *So Joshua fought the Amalekites as Moses had ordered, and Moses, Aaron and Hur went to the top of the hill. As long as Moses held up his hands, the Israelites were winning, but whenever he lowered his hands, the Amalekites were winning. When Moses' hands grew tired, they took a stone and put it under him and he sat on it. Aaron and Hur held his hands up—one on one side, one on the other—so that his hands remained steady till sunset. So Joshua overcame the Amalekite army with the sword.*

The key characteristics of Amalek are apparent from the biblical description above. This was a battle between the descendants of Jacob and Esau. Although it was Moses' war, Joshua was the one to actually fight. This was a matter of lineage. Joshua was a descendant of Joseph (and Jacob), while Amalek was a member of Esau's family. This battle, like all the other Amalek battles, fulfilled the prophecy in Obadiah: *"The house of Jacob will be as fire and the house of Joseph as the flame, while the house of Esau will be as straw."*[28]

In addition, it was a super-rational battle. The success of the battle depended on the raised hands of Moses. This is because Amalek attacks without any explanation or cause. To combat Amalek, one must reach beyond reason, to a place within oneself where rational thoughts are irrelevant. This is the significance of Moses raising his hands above his head.[29]

Moses was instructed[30] to record the commandment to exterminate the nation of Amalek only after the battle, for fulfillment of the Divine Purpose was not yet possible. Thus, the conflict continues: *"God maintains a struggle with Amalek, from generation to generation."*[31]

In the time of King Saul, about 450 years later, prior to the building of the First Temple, the time had come to annihilate Amalek. One day, Samuel (a prophet) came to King Saul with a demand from God to wage war against the nation of Amalek and destroy it completely. King Saul was told to show no pity. Nothing was to remain of the entire nation and all its wealth, for as long as there were any Amalekites alive, there could be no peace for Israel. King Saul set out with an army of *"two hundred thousand foot soldiers and ten thousand from Judah"*[32] and met the enemy in the valley near their main city. After a bitter battle, the army of Amalek was annihilated, and the inhabitants of the city were put to death. None escaped alive except their king, Agag, on whom Saul took pity,[33] thus allowing the nation of Amalek to perpetuate. King Saul's mistake cost him his throne and allowed the conflict with Amalek to continue.

Another battle with Amalek arose again 500 years later, prior to the building of the Second Temple. At that time, the Jews were subjects of the mighty Persian Empire, which ruled over significant portions of the ancient world and spanned segments of three continents: Asia, Europe, and Africa. The story of this battle with Amalek is recorded in the Book of Esther. Haman, the main antagonist in the Book of Esther, was a vizier in the Persian Empire under King Ahasuerus and a descendant of King Agag. Haman approached King Ahasuerus and received permission to exterminate the Jews. Haman sent proclamations throughout the entire empire. These proclamations, sealed with the royal signet ring, ordered the people to rise up against the Jews and kill them all—men, women, and children. Through a series of events, including fasting and praying by the whole Jewish population, Esther managed to avert the genocide. Once again, the attempted genocide was illogical and instigated by a descendant of Amalek.

Sources[34] teach that the nation of Amalek will continue to derive from Haman. Today, although the nation of Amalek definitely and unfortunately exists, we cannot say with certainty who they are or where they exist. In the future, in the End of Days, the nation of Amalek will be eradicated in its entirety so that the Divine Purpose can be fulfilled.[35] The battle with Amalek is one instance of history repeating itself.

Now that we understand what stands in the way of reaching the end goal—how and when do we get there?

Chapter 3

The Messianic Era

Given the obstacles to achieving the Cosmic Purpose, is the Messianic Era (which ushers in the Cosmic Purpose) guaranteed or conditional? Is there a set time frame?

It is absolutely guaranteed to happen, despite our behavior and despite whatever final attempt Amalek may make to stop it. The ultimate time for the 'end' is unconditional; it does not depend on our merit or on Amalek's efforts to sabotage it, as it is said, *"For My* [God's] *own sake, for My own sake, I will do it"*;[1] *"I wrought for My Name's sake that it should not be profaned in the eyes of the nations."*[2]

The actual default date for the Messianic age is unknown to humans.[3] The time is predetermined from the beginning of Creation: *"in its time I will hasten it."*[4] *"In its time"* means a set date, predetermined from the beginning of Creation.[5] However, this date, which as we have seen from the biblical timeline must occur prior to the year 6000, is the default date. If we merit it, God *"will hasten it,"* meaning it will occur before its time.[6] We shall see later that in the course of history there have been special times when the Messianic Era could have been expedited.

We will now examine the description of both the time just before the End of Days and that of the actual End of Days. We will only review a very high-level summary and some key prophecies, because our main purpose is to understand the default process and timeline of the End of Days, not only by relying on prophecies, but also by analyzing the overall pattern of history, and by studying how past and present fit into this pattern. We will also examine some of the key prophecies about those who will lead the world to its destination, so we can recognize not just the pattern of the End of Days process, but also the players.

The Time Preceding the End of Days

The precursor to the last section of the glass maze is very confusing. There are many mirrors, making the end seem distant, creating an illusion of several paths, and leading to false turns and uncertainties along the way.

There prevails a singular harmony among the apocalyptic writings and traditions, revealing that the final redemption shall be preceded by great distress, darkness, and moral decline. *"When you see a generation ever dwindling, hope for him* [the Messiah] . . . *when you see a generation overwhelmed by many troubles as by a river, await him."*[7] This period is described as the travail (i.e., painful or laborious effort) of the pre-Messianic time.

The social conditions describing the period prior to the End of Days sound very familiar. At the personal and family level, the accelerated pace of change will lead to parents and children growing up in different eras, and thus traditions typically passed from parents to children will be largely lost:[8]

> *insolence will increase and honour dwindle; . . . youths will put old men to shame, the old will stand up in the presence of the young, a son will revile his father, a daughter will rise against her mother, a daughter-in-law against her mother-in-law, and a man's enemies will be the members of his household; a son will not feel ashamed before his father.*[9]

At the societal level, we will experience:

> *oppressing inflation; unbridled irresponsibility on the part of authorities; centers of learning becoming bawdy houses; . . . impudent leadership.*[10]

> *. . . famines; mutual denunciations; epidemics of terrible diseases;*
> *poverty and scarcity; cursing and blaspheming; [and] international*
> *confrontations—nations provoking and fighting each other.*[11]

But it's not only doom and gloom. Many positives also will abound: "*a good measure of prosperity*";[12] scientific and technological discoveries and advances;[13] a manifestation and propagation of the mystical teachings of the Torah.[14]

Finally, there are numerous traditions that as a prelude to the Messiah, Jews will begin to return to resettle the Land of Israel with a measure of political independence.[15] There is also a tradition, based on the prophecy of Ezekiel, that the land will be cultivated at that time: "*You mountains of Israel give forth your branches and bear your fruit for My people Israel, for they are close to returning.*"[16]

Prophecies about the End of Days

The final part of the maze is clearer. There are a few turns as we approach the exit, with few if any options—we have to just follow the path. However, we cannot be sure of which path until we get there. One thing we do know is that it will happen, and it's unconditional:

> *Thus said the Lord God: I am not doing (this) for your sake,*
> *House of Israel, but for My holy Name which you profaned among*
> *the nations whither you came. I shall sanctify My great Name . . .*
> *and the nations shall know that I am God, says the Lord God.* [17]

The main tenets of the End of Days are elaborated in the Books of Isaiah, Jeremiah, and Ezekiel. As discussed earlier, the exact meaning and order of occurrence are sources of much discussion. The following are the main events—perhaps in the right order, perhaps not:

The coming of the Messiah:

> *I see it, but not now; I behold it, but not soon. A star* [the Messiah] *has gone forth from Jacob, and a staff will arise from Israel which will crush the princes of Moab and uproot all the sons of Seth* [all humanity].[18]

God sends the Messiah, son of (ben) Joseph, who sets the stage, followed by the Messiah, son of David, who leads the world and ushers in an age of justice and peace, which we will discuss in the next section.

The Battle of Gog and Magog.[19] This will be a climactic battle against the forces of evil,[20] in the early stages of the Messianic Era. These evil forces (Gog and Magog) will presumptuously undertake to battle not only Israel but the Almighty Himself and will suffer an appropriate defeat:

> *I [God] have many messengers whom I can send into battle. But the war against Gog and Magog I shall wage Myself. Their destruction shall be complete.*[21]

Even so, for a while, it will be a most traumatic event with great trials and tribulations for Israel. As this event is shrouded in mystery, we are uncertain as to the identity of Gog and Magog, and whether this battle will be physical, or spiritual or both.

The redemption of Israel from exile and the return of the Jewish people to the Land of Israel.[22] The ingathering of the exiles from the Diaspora, including the 10 "Lost Tribes," will be complete:[23]

> *I [God] shall take you out from the nations and gather you from the lands in which you were scattered . . . For on My holy mountain, on the mountain of the height of Israel, says the Lord*

God, there shall all of the whole House of Israel serve Me . . . when I bring you out from the nations and gather you from the lands where you were scattered, and I shall be sanctified in you in the eyes of the nations. You shall know that I am God when I bring you to the earth of Israel, to the land about which I raised My hand to give it to your fathers.[24]

The restoration of the House of David and the Temple in Jerusalem:

I shall give My Sanctuary in their midst forever. My dwelling-place shall be over them . . . The nations shall know that I am God who sanctifies Israel, when My Sanctuary shall be in the midst of them forever.[25]

The rebuilt Third Temple in Jerusalem will be the central focus of all humanity—as Isaiah says, *"My home will be considered a 'House of Prayer' for all the nations."*[26]

The recognition of God by all nations. The Messiah will rule over all of humanity with kindness and justice, upholding the Seven Noahide Laws for humankind at large and the 613 commandments of the Torah for Jews. He will also be the ultimate teacher and the conduit through which the deepest and most profound dimensions of spirituality will be revealed by God.

God shall be King over the entire earth. In that day God shall be One and His Name One.[27] *The earth shall be full of knowledge of God as the waters cover the sea.*[28]

The resurrection of the dead.[29] The body will be resurrected, and the soul will be reunited with the body.[30] The first hint that the dead will be resurrected comes from the book of Exodus. God promised the Land of Israel to the Patriarchs, yet the promise went unfulfilled in their lifetimes:

ROADMAP TO THE END OF DAYS

> *And I [God] revealed Myself to Abraham, to Isaac, and to Jacob . . . And I have also established My covenant with them, to give them the Land of Canaan, the land of their dwellings, where they dwelled.*[31]

Since the promise went unfulfilled in their lifetimes, it will be fulfilled after they are resurrected.[32]

More explicit references to the resurrection of the dead are found in the Books of Isaiah and Ezekiel:

> *Your dead shall be revived, my corpses shall arise; awaken and sing you who dwell in the dust, for a dew of lights is your dew. . . .*[33] *Behold I will open your graves and raise you from your graves, My people; and I will bring you into the Land of Israel . . . My people. I shall put My spirit into you and you will live, and I will place you upon your land, and you will know that I, God, have spoken and done, says God.*[34]

Finally, the resurrected will be healed:

> *Just as a person goes, so he will return. If he died blind, deaf or mute, he will return blind, deaf or mute. As he goes clothed, he will return clothed. God said, "let them rise as they went—and afterwards I will heal them."*[35]

Universal peace and the ushering in of the seventh millennium. The era will witness ultimate physical and spiritual bliss:

> *In the days of the Mashiach man will return to what he was before the sin of Adam, when by his nature he did what should properly be done [good], and there were no conflicting desires in his will . . . the heart will not desire the improper and it will have no craving whatever for it [for evil].*[36] *And at that time there will be no hunger or war, no jealousy or rivalry. For the good will be plentiful,*

28

and all delicacies available as dust. The entire occupation of the world will be only to know God. . . .[37] *The eyes of the blind shall be clear-sighted, and the ears of the deaf shall be opened . . . the lame shall leap as a hart and the tongue of the dumb shall sing. . . .*[38] *Death shall be swallowed up forever and God shall wipe the tears from every face. . . .*[39] *Strangers shall stand and feed your flocks and aliens shall be your plowmen and your vinedressers.*[40]

The Messiahs

Yes, 'Messiahs' is not a misprint; as in many situations, someone sets the stage to achieve a goal, and someone else achieves it. Most Jewish sources interpret Scriptures to imply that the Messiah ben Joseph will come first.

The essential task of Messiah ben Joseph is to act as precursor to Messiah ben David, for whose coming he will prepare the world. Various sources attribute to him different functions.[41] However, the principal and final function ascribed to Messiah ben Joseph is of a political and military nature. He shall wage war against the forces of evil that oppress Israel. Post-battle there will be a period of great calamities,[42] and thereafter Messiah ben David shall come and inaugurate the Messianic Era of everlasting peace and bliss. Messiah ben David[43] will fulfill all the prophecies of the End of Days not completed by Messiah ben Joseph.

How are we to recognize Messiah ben David when he comes? The sources indicate those things the Messiah will not do, those he does not have to do, and those he must do:

He will not change anything in the Torah: "*do not add to what I command you and do not subtract from it, but keep the commands of the Lord your God that I give you.*"[44]

He will not have to perform signs and wonders and bring about novel things in the world.[45]

He will have to fulfill the prophecies of the End of Days:[46]

> *If a king arises from the House of David who meditates on the Torah and occupies himself with the commandments . . . he will prevail upon all of Israel to walk in and strengthen its breaches, and he will fight the battles of God—it may be assumed that he is Mashiach [Messiah]. If he did [these things] successfully and defeated all the nations around him, built the Sanctuary on its site and gathered the dispersed of Israel—he is definitely Mashiach! If he did not succeed to that extent or was killed, it is clear that he is not the Mashiach.*

In short, we will only recognize Messiah ben David in hindsight, once he has completed almost all the End of Days prophecies outlined in the prior section.

This very brief description of events and personalities provides the background for what lies ahead. We must now try to stand above the maze, discover the pattern of the Divine Plan, place historical events in context, and revisit the above prophecies in this new light to see whether we can understand the recent past and glimpse the future. We now turn to the Universal Timeline, the pattern of the Divine Plan of history—that is, the default pattern. Yes, default pattern; remember, we can change the course. But will we?

Chapter 4

The Universal Timeline

When we create, we turn an abstract idea into a real object in our finite world. To make a house, we start with a picture in our mind, then we set out a scale on a piece of paper or in a computer file and draw a blueprint representing the house. We later use the blueprint to measure and build the actual physical structure.

We are made in *"the image of God,"*[1] which, among other implications, also indicates that our creative process is like His.[2] Thus, God set out a blueprint, the Torah, to create the finite world and guide to history.[3] How do we read His blueprint? Its scale is time. The events described in it are placed on a timeline. But what is the pattern, the underlying methodology, of how the timeline is laid out? The pattern of the timeline is based on the channels of Divine energy, the sefirot.[4]

The Sefirot

In the mystical tradition we are told that God contracts His infinity through ten channels of Divine energy, or life force, the sefirot (singular sefirah). If we look closely, the Creation is designed around some or all of these sefirot. For example, physical arrangements such as our ten fingers and toes, and more abstract concepts such as the 10 Commandments and the ten plagues, correspond to the ten sefirot (see Figure 4.1).

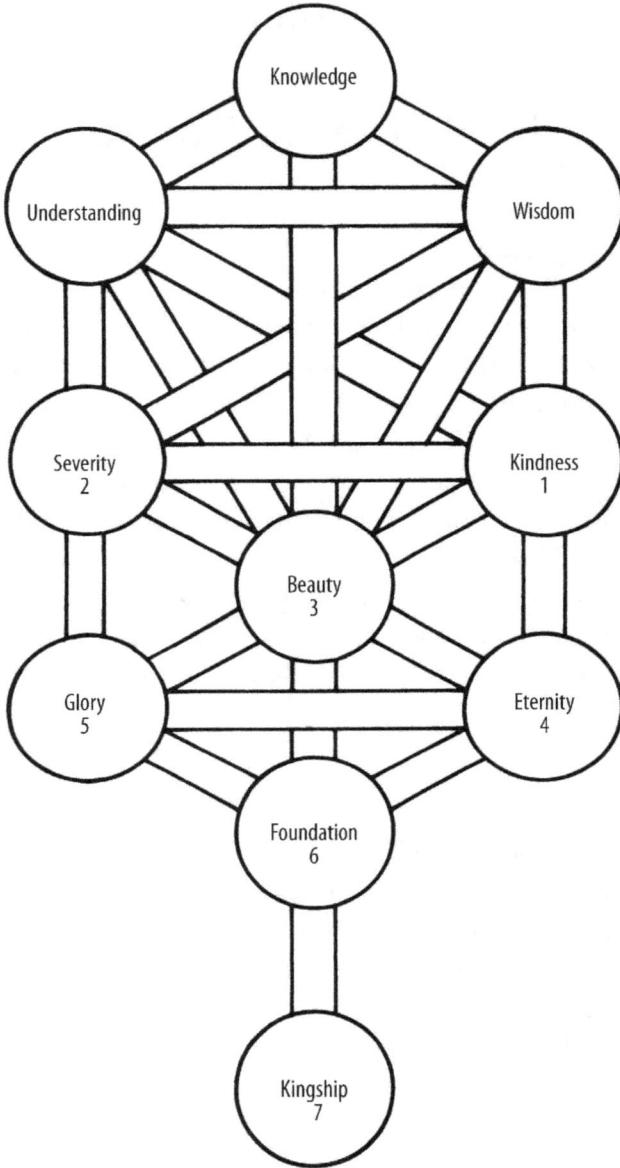

Figure 4.1   The Ten Sefirot

Appendix B delves into the sefirot in some detail, as well as patterns of ten, seven and six, and I urge you to read it. What we need to understand for the moment is the correspondence between the sefirot, their manifestation in physical time, and the patterns of biblical history.

The ten sefirot are usually numbered from 1 to 10, starting at the top right. However, since the first three sefirot, associated with the mind (wisdom, understanding, and knowledge), do not manifest themselves in physical time they are not assigned a number in this book. In the realm of physical time, only the lower seven of the ten sefirot manifest. These are associated with emotions: kindness, severity, beauty, eternity, glory, foundation and kingship, which in this book are numbered from 1 to 7.

Accordingly, we have the 6 Days of Creation, followed by the seventh day, in which God abstained from Creation. Sefirot one through seven match a corresponding Creation day. Each week in this world is a reflection of the original Creation week, with six days of work or other creative endeavors and one day of rest. In turn, we have the six years we work the land, followed by the seventh year, the sabbatical year of rest for the land.[5] And, as we have seen, we have 6,000 years of biblical history, followed by the seventh millennium.

Thus, time and history proceed in patterns of seven: at the microscopic level of each seven-day week and at the macroscopic level of seven millennia. These patterns of seven are parallel to each other, since they all emanate from the same seven sefirot.

The millennia of history also mirror the original Creation week. Each Creation day corresponds to one of the six millennia and the Sabbath to the seventh millennium,[6] as illustrated in Figure 4.2.

Creation Day	World Events	
	Gregorian calendar (year)	Biblical Calendar (year)
	3760 BCE	1
Day 1 Sunday	Life of Adam	
	2761 BCE	1000
Day 2 Monday	Time of Noah	
	1761 BCE	2000
Day 3 Tuesday	Formation of the Nation of Israel Giving of the Torah King David ruled	
	761 BCE	3000
Day 4 Wednesday	Two Temples stood	
	240 CE	4000
Day 5 Thursday	Population expansion without rule Beginning of fourth and current exile	
	1240 CE	5000
Day 6 Friday	Secular kingdoms and wars End of Days, culminating with the Resurrection of the Dead	
	2240 CE	6000
Day 7 Saturday	First stage of the World to Come	
	3240 CE	7000

Figure 4.2   Basic Timeline of World History

Thus, Creation days, biblical time, and Common Era time correspond as follows:

The first day of Creation (Sunday) corresponds to the first millennium of biblical history (i.e., the first 1,000 biblical years or years 1 to 1000) or years 3760 BCE to 2761 BCE.

The second day of Creation corresponds to the second millennium of biblical history (years 1001 to 2000) or years 2760 BCE to 1761 BCE.

The third day of Creation corresponds to the third millennium of biblical history (years 2001 to 3000) or years 1760 BCE to 761 BCE.

The fourth day of Creation corresponds to the fourth millennium of biblical history (years 3001 to 4000) or years 760 BCE to 240 CE.

The fifth day of Creation corresponds to the fifth millennium of biblical history (years 4001 to 5000) or years 241 CE to 1240 CE.

The sixth day of Creation corresponds to the sixth millennium of biblical history (years 5001 to 6000) or years 1241 CE to 2240 CE.

With this knowledge, we have enough background to examine the very general pattern of biblical history. Once we have glimpsed this general pattern, I will further elaborate on the relationship between the sefirot and time, in order to examine the pattern of history as it relates to specific critical periods in which the Divine Purpose may be fulfilled.

The General Pattern of Biblical History

The Bible is not a history book; nonetheless, it contains a chronology from Creation through the first several thousand years. Beyond that we follow the chronicle of the nation of Israel to modern times to obtain a "biblical timeline of history." A brief summary of the major events in this timeline is shown in Appendix A, Table A.1 Historical Summary.

Nachmanides—also known as Rabbi Moses ben Nachman Girondi, Bonastrucça Porta, and by his acronym Ramban[7] (Gerona, 1194–Land of Israel, 1270 CE)—was a leading medieval scholar, rabbi, philosopher, physician and biblical commentator. In his commentary on Genesis, he advances the view that the 6 Days of Creation parallel the 6,000 years of biblical history,[8] as discussed above. The full text of his analysis is contained in Appendix C. He draws a parallel showing how the major events in each day of Creation are reflected in each of the millennia:

The first day of Creation, when God made light, corresponds to the life of Adam, who in the first millennium (he lived almost 1,000 years) was to be a light to the world.

The second day of Creation, when God separated the upper and lower waters, corresponds to the time of Noah in the second millennium, when the waters of the flood separated the righteous from the wicked.

The third day of Creation, when the Earth was made (which would later, on the sixth day, house the key Creation, humanity), corresponds to the time of building the nation of Israel, from Abraham through David, in the third millennium.

The fourth day of Creation, when the sun and the moon were made, corresponds to when the two Temples (the spiritual luminaries) stood, during the fourth millennium.

The fifth day of Creation, when the waters swarmed with living creatures, corresponds to the fifth millennium, when the population expanded without much rule or stability.

The sixth day of Creation, in the morning, when the beasts of the field were made, corresponds to a period of domination by secular kingdoms and violent wars. The completion of Adam, his subsequent sin and his expulsion from the garden in the afternoon of Day 6 correspond to late in the sixth millennium, which will therefore culminate with humans correcting Adam's sin, in the End of Days, and ushering in the seventh millennium.

Are all of the above coincidence or due to design? It is hard to tell when looking at generalities, so let's now look at specifics.

The Specific Pattern of History

We have seen that time obeys certain cycles, and in particular, that history proceeds through six millennia corresponding to the 6 Days of Creation. But what can we infer about each millennium? Is there a pattern of time and history within each one? Yes. And are millennia related to each other within similar periods of history? Yes.

Not only is each millennium related to one of the sefirot and to one of the Creation days; the 1,000 years of each millennium is also divided into six equal parts related to each of those sefirot. In other words, the 6,000 years of history break down into 36 periods of approximately 167 years.* The reason for this is explained in detail and with extensive references in Appendix B.

---

* Six periods of 1,000 years, with each 1,000-year period divided into six periods of approximately 167 years each—i.e., 1,000 divided by six is approximately 167.

Briefly, the idea that history is divided into 36 equal periods is based on the biblical concept of completion. We count six years plus the sabbatical year to complete a sabbatical cycle.[9] In general, completion comes by including all of the sefirot manifest in each other, so that every part reflects all the other parts.[10] Therefore, we count seven sabbatical cycles—seven times seven years, or 49 years—to reach the completion of the cycle, the 50th year, which Leviticus calls the Jubilee Year.[11] In history, however, where only six sefirot manifest, the cycle of six (corresponding to the 6,000 years of history) becomes complete with a cycle of six times six, or 36 periods of time (each approximately 167 years).

Cosmically, we are used to very regular cycles of time. We have the day defined by the Earth's rotation, we have the month defined by the moon orbiting the Earth, and we have the year defined by the Earth circling the sun. Nonetheless, the Bible tells us to follow a pattern of seven days per week, which is not tied to the motion of a cosmic body. We run our lives on this weekly pattern, and the weeks fit within the overall cosmic calendar of months, seasons, and years.

Similarly, the Bible indicates that history proceeds in periods of 167 years; six of these make a millennium, and six millennia make the full span of biblical history (6,000 years), followed by the seventh millennium. Each of the 36 periods of history is unique yet also related to other periods in very specific ways. History does have a pattern and 'repeats' itself.

How do we decipher this pattern of history? How do we focus on the really important or critical periods? To decipher the pattern, we have to understand how periods of history relate to each other. It helps to look at the example of our daily life, in which we find patterns between similar periods of time. For many of us, all Mondays are filled with similar activities, as are Saturdays, and so on. Furthermore, to rest on Saturday we have to make some preparations on Fridays. Thus, in our week there is a relation from one day to the other, and also between the same days of different weeks. Also, the days when special or critical things happen are more important than others; for example, we are more likely to devote Saturday or Sunday to the family than Monday.

In the case of history, the pattern is designed from the outset. Each of the six millennia corresponds to a sefirah and a Creation day. This establishes the function of a particular millennium and also its relationship to other millennia. Furthermore, each millennium is divided into six periods that, in turn, correspond to a Creation day and a sefirah; in this way, they are related to similar periods in other millennia. Table 4.1 illustrates this correspondence using biblical years.

The six millennia proceed in columns from left to right, and each millennium is divided into six equal periods, shown in the rows. Look, for example, at the third-millennium column and the first-period cell within that column; this indicates the biblical years 2001 to 2167. Similarly, the sixth-millennium column has a fifth-period cell for the biblical years 5667 to 5883 (which are 1907 to 2073 CE[12]).

Table 4.1 Historical Timeline in Biblical Years

| Period | Millennium | | | | | |
	1st	2nd	3rd	4th	5th	6th
1st	1–167	1001–1167	2001–2167	3001–3167	4001–4167	5001–5167
2nd	167–333	1167–1333	2167–2333	3167–3333	4167–4333	5167–5333
3rd	333–500	1333–1500	2333–2550	3333–3500	4333–4500	5333–5500
4th	501–667	1501–1667	2501–2667	3501–3667	4501–4667	5501–5667
5th	667–833	1667–1833	2667–2833	3667–3833	4667–4833	5667–5833
6th	833–1000	1833–2000	2833–3000	3833–4000	4833–5000	5833–6000

Note: The dark gray and light gray highlighted years indicate critical periods.

To understand the relationships between the different 167-year periods of history, we must understand the parallel relationship between the 6 Days of Creation and then apply this relationship to the corresponding six millennia and six periods within each millennium. Appendix B elaborates upon the essential information presented in Table 4.2.

Table 4.2 The Parallel Pattern of Creation Days

Day 1: Light	→	**Day 4:** Sun & Moon
Day 2: Separation of the waters	→	**Day 5:** Life in the waters
Day 3: Earth	→	**Day 6:** Life on Earth

As we can see, the six Creation days consist of two parallel patterns of three days. Day 1 corresponds to Day 4, Day 2 corresponds to Day 5, and Day 3 corresponds to Day 6. For example,[13] in Day 1 there was light; in Day 4 came the sun (and the moon). Day 1 is the necessary initial creation, just light (i.e., electromagnetic radiation); Day 4 is light manifest in a more usable form, the sun. Similarly,[14] Day 3 is the creation of the Earth (necessary for life to exist), and Day 6 is the creation of life on Earth.

Millennia correspond in the same way. For example, the third millennium is parallel to the sixth millennium. In particular, we will see that the Divine Purpose is set up in the third millennium (with the giving of the law at Sinai), and it is concluded with the End of Days in the sixth millennium.

The six periods within each millennium also correspond in the same way. For example, the third period in each millennium is parallel to the sixth period—that is, the same kinds of events repeat themselves in these two periods.

The times where critical events of history are scheduled to occur are related to Day 3 and Day 6, corresponding in turn to the purpose of Creationè first, the creation of the Earth (Day 3), and then the creation of humans on Earth (Day 6): *"I made the earth and created man upon it."*[15]

Thus, if we look again at Table 4.1, we see that the third period of the third millennium (years 2333 to 2500, in dark gray) is the first critical period and therefore the key formative period for the fulfillment of the Divine Purpose. This period corresponds to the Exodus and the giving of the law (year 2448). Similarly, the fulfillment of the Divine mission manifests during the sixth period of the sixth millennium (years 5833 to 6000, also in dark gray, which are 2073 to 2240 CE).

There are three more critical periods (in light gray, as explained in Appendix B). Two of these correspond to the times of the First and Second Temples, respectively. The third critical period, as we shall see later, was a missed opportunity to build a Temple.

Four of the five[16] critical periods in history have already occurred, and we have the detailed times and description of the events that transpired during these periods. Since all of the critical periods are parallel, we are able to discover the pattern and then extend it to the upcoming last critical period (the End of Days) in order to ascertain which events will happen and when.

Just before the critical periods are preparatory periods (just as, for example, some of us prepare on Friday to rest on Saturday). We are now completing the preparatory period for the End of Days: the fifth period of the sixth millennium (1907 to 2073 CE). By looking at prior parallel preparatory periods we can understand the meaning of what has happened in the past 100 years and how that is ushering in the End of Days.

The remainder of this book is devoted to studying the timing and meaning of historical events that occurred in prior preparatory and critical periods so we can ascertain the meaning of present-day events and the outlook for the future.

Chapter 5

The Rhythm of History: Looking Back

> Rhythm: A sequence of regularly recurring functions or events.

In Chapter 4, we looked at the pattern of history to try to identify critical periods when significant and decisive events occurred in relation to achieving the Divine Purpose and reaching the End of Days—i.e., the conclusion of the Divine Plan. We determined that four critical periods have already passed.

In this chapter, we will examine these previous periods in detail in order to discern the rhythm of history. In the first critical period, the Divine Plan was set up. We should find that the next three critical periods were eras when the End of Days could have occurred but did not.

If we look again at Table 4.1, zeroing in on the dark gray areas in the third millennium and the light gray areas in the third and fourth millennia, these four critical periods occurred during the following times:

Divine Plan is set up
1st critical period: biblical years 2333 to 2500
(1428 to 1261 BCE)

1st opportunity for conclusion of the Divine Plan
2nd critical period: biblical years 2833 to 3000
(928 to 761 BCE)

2ⁿᵈ opportunity for conclusion of the Divine Plan
3ʳᵈ critical period: biblical years 3333 to 3500
(428 to 261 BCE)

3ʳᵈ opportunity for conclusion of the Divine Plan
4ᵗʰ critical period: biblical years 3833 to 4000
(72 to 239 CE)

Before continuing with the detailed analysis of key events and their timing, we will briefly review what happened in each of these periods.

Overview of Key Periods

In Chapter 1, we reviewed the overall biblical timeline of history. We now focus more closely on the first preparatory period and the four critical periods. At any time you can refer to Appendix A, as it provides a summary of the historical timeline that contains many of the key events we will be discussing.

1ˢᵀ PREPARATORY PERIOD

The preparation for the Divine Plan to be set up begins in the year 2000, with Abraham recognizing the existence of one God and smashing his father's idols.[1] Preparation continues (2167–2332)[2] with Jacob obtaining his father Isaac's blessing, instead of his brother Esau, initiating the ages-old conflict. To avoid being killed by Esau, Jacob goes into exile, later marrying and having 11 children before returning and confronting his brother. He then has his 12ᵗʰ child, Benjamin.

The brothers conspire against Jacob's favorite son, Joseph, who as a result is sold into slavery in Egypt.

Once he is in Egypt, his ability to interpret dreams brings him to Pharaoh's attention, and he is asked to interpret a troubling dream that foretells seven years of plenty followed by years of famine.

Pharaoh is so impressed that he appoints Joseph Viceroy to oversee preparations for the upcoming famine. Joseph manages the affairs of Egypt during the years of plenty and the subsequent years of famine.[3]

Meanwhile, Jacob and the rest of his family exhaust their supplies during the famine years and are forced to go to Egypt, where Joseph has prepared for them. Due to Joseph's position and the respect he garners, Jacob and his descendants—the Israelites—live in relatively prosperous times. However, once Jacob and all his sons have died, as has the pharaoh who appointed Joseph, the new pharaoh enslaves all the children of Israel except the tribe of Levi.[4]

Thus, the preparatory period ends in disaster. As we shall see, disaster/disruption always seems to be a prerequisite for the new birth occurring in the subsequent critical period.

THE DIVINE PLAN IS SET UP:
1ST CRITICAL PERIOD (2333–2500)[5]

During the slavery era, Pharaoh becomes concerned that in the event of a war, Hebrew males may join the Egyptians' enemies.[6] He therefore commands that all male Hebrew children be killed. When Moses is born, his mother hides him among the reeds by the river, where he is discovered by Pharaoh's daughter. He grows up under her care, but later, when he kills an Egyptian slave master who is beating a Hebrew to death, he is forced to flee Egypt to assure his safety.

God determines that it is time to end the Israelites' slavery and that Moses will be his agent, so He appears to Moses and commands him to lead the children of Israel out of Egypt to the land of Canaan (the Promised Land); this is known as the Exodus. The key events of the Exodus (which ensue in rapid progression over a relatively short time) are as follows:[7]

In 2447, God appears to Moses in a burning bush and commands him to free the Israelites.

God then sends 10 plagues upon Egypt, and the Israelites leave in 2448.

Amalek, the eternal enemy of the Israelites, launches an unprovoked attack to try to stop their progress.[8]

The Israelites are able to cross the Sea of Reeds when Moses parts the water; the pursuing Egyptians are drowned, leaving the Israelites fully free.

At Mount Sinai, still in 2448, Moses receives the first Tablets (containing the 10 Commandments)[9] and the Torah. After smashing the Tablets in anger because he finds the Israelites worshipping an idol (the Golden Calf), he receives the second Tablets in 2449. Both the first broken Tablets and the second intact Tablets are kept in the Holy Ark of the Covenant.

Still in the wilderness, in 2449 the Israelites erect the Tabernacle, a dwelling place for the Divine.[10] Almost 40 years later, following Moses' death, the children of Israel cross the Jordan River and enter the Promised Land.

1ST OPPORTUNITY FOR CONCLUSION OF THE DIVINE PLAN:
2ND CRITICAL PERIOD (2833–3000)[11]

Once in the Promised Land and after the death of Joshua, the Israelites are independent in their own homeland and for the first time do not have a single, strong leader. Without a central figure, there is a lack of religious authority and almost continual warfare.

Just prior to the second critical period, the Israelites are being oppressed by the Philistines, so God appoints Samson to rescue them. Samson has amazing strength, but to keep this strength he must never cut his hair. For many years, Samson makes progress in his mission to rescue his people, despite numerous setbacks. He marries a Philistine woman named Delilah, who had converted to Judaism. However, Delilah is bribed by the Philistines to find out the secret to Samson's strength. Then, as he sleeps, she cuts off his hair, enabling him to be captured and blinded. As the Philistines are celebrating their victory in a great hall, Samson makes a last appeal to God for strength and brings the roof crashing down, killing all of them as well as himself.

Hence, the disruptive event preceding the second critical period is Samson's failure to achieve his mission. His death leads to conquest by the Philistines, the eventual capture of the Holy Ark, and the destruction of the Tabernacle.[12]

The critical period then begins with Saul being appointed King. Saul is commanded to battle against and exterminate Amalek—thus, this is the first opportunity to fulfill the Divine Plan. Saul fails to wipe out all of them, but he does win the war, setting the stage for the next key steps of the historical plan to unfold.

David then becomes King. Among many other accomplishments, he provides the supplies and instructions for building the First Temple, a task that his son, King Solomon, accomplishes. Following the death of Solomon, the kingdom is divided due to poor leadership, unrest, and subsequent invasions. Hence, the Divine Plan is not concluded.

2ND OPPORTUNITY FOR CONCLUSION OF THE DIVINE PLAN:
3RD CRITICAL PERIOD (3333–3500)[13]

After the kingdom is divided, the unrest continues, the tribes are exiled, and eventually the final siege of Jerusalem ensues. Then, just prior to this third critical period, the First Temple is destroyed by the Neo-Babylonian King Nebuchadnezzar II, marking the disruptive event that precedes the third critical period. Soon after, key personalities are born and move into leadership roles, including Ezra[14] and Esther.[15] Then there is another successful battle with Amalek—although Amalek still is not exterminated—recorded in the book of Esther, followed by the completion of the Second Temple.

Jews begin returning from exile, led by Ezra the scribe, who emphasizes adherence to religious principles. They are followed by Nehemiah,[16] who rebuilds the walls of Jerusalem. By 3448, Ezra has published the 24 books of the written Torah and dies. The good times do not last, as Alexander the Great, who conquered Persia, expands into the region, bringing with him the Greek culture in which he was raised. A period of Greek cultural domination ensues, leading (amongst other things) to the Bible being translated into Greek. Once again, the Divine Plan is not concluded.

3RD OPPORTUNITY FOR CONCLUSION OF THE DIVINE PLAN:
4TH CRITICAL PERIOD (3833–4000)[17]

Under Greek cultural domination there is a brief respite as the Maccabees[18] lead a revolt (celebrated as Hanukah today). However, by 3700 the Romans take control of the area. Events then unfold such that the Second Temple is destroyed by the Romans after a Jewish rebellion in 3829, marking the disruptive event that precedes the fourth critical period. Soon, key leaders arise, such as Bar Kokhba, who was the leader of the final and most successful Jewish rebellion against Rome, in 3893 (133 CE).[19] There is growing momentum to regain control from the Romans and rebuild the Temple, but this time the war against Amalek (Bar Kokhba versus Rome) is lost. Thus, the Divine Plan once again is not concluded.

Following the defeat of Bar Kokhba, the Romans ban Judaism. Nonetheless, the political climate does improve; the Romans become confident that Jews are no longer a threat, so they allow work to continue on compiling the Oral tradition in written form. This period ends with the completion of the final editing of the Mishna, the key component of the Talmud, by Rabbi Yehudah HaNasi, who was part of the royal line descended from King David.[20]

Analyzing the Rhythm of History

In analyzing the rhythm of history, we must constantly remind ourselves that there is a Divine Plan dictating a definite time for every particular event. We will call this its default time. However, humans have free will, so we control the exact timing of when events actually occur. Thus, events will happen around but not exactly at their default time.

When we look at two similar events—say, the building of each of the two Temples—we should not expect them to fall right at the same place in the pattern, the default time; instead, we should expect their occurrence to vary slightly from the default time.

What is the default time? By and large, we don't know. However, now that we have determined the pattern of history (i.e., the cosmic design), we can populate it with the historical events just reviewed and, based on when similar events occurred, estimate their default time.

Note that there are a few exceptions when Scripture tells us the exact time something is supposed to take place, and even the deviation to when it actually happened. One example is when Joseph was released from prison to become the Viceroy of Egypt—a critical moment in the assurance of the formation of the nation. The sources tell us that he was freed exactly two years after the time designated for his release (the default time).[21] The postponement resulted from a misjudgment by Joseph, who therefore temporarily delayed this event of the Divine Plan by two years.[22]

Looking Back

We will now begin to populate these past periods with the actual events that occurred. Table 5.1 helps us to organize them.

Each of the first four columns in Table 5.1 contains the key historical events, with their (biblical) year of occurrence. The rows designate years in increments of 10 (with some rows omitted where no significant events occurred).

The table summarizes the events occurring at the end of the preparatory periods, as well the events occurring during each of the critical periods. The far right column, entitled Pattern, provides a label that summarizes key events within the associated corresponding rows: Disruptive Event; Birth of Leader; Leader Becomes King, Amalek Battle; Building of Temple and New Revelation; and Death of Leader.

A very clear pattern emerges when we compare equivalent periods of history—that is, across the first four columns.

Disruptive Event. Each critical period is preceded (at the end of the preparatory period) by a major disruptive event: slavery, conquest and the Temples' destruction. These disruptions all start or happen during a particular time and can last (e.g., slavery) or produce disruptive effects that last (e.g., conquest and no existing Temple) well into the critical period.

Birth of Leader. Each critical period begins with the birth of key figures, either a prophet from the priestly tribe, or a king, or both: the birth of Moses, David, Ezra,[23] and Bar Kokhba.[24] Note that where we don't have exact birth dates, the birth date is estimated based on later events and displayed with a question mark.

Leader Becomes King, Amalek Battle. When the leader matures, he becomes the king; in times without kings, he assumes another leadership position. Soon thereafter, he is faced with a religious challenge and a battle with Amalek. Moses battles Amalek after the nation leaves Egypt.[25] Saul battles Amalek before the building of the First Temple. Just before the completion of the Second Temple, there is another battle with Amalek, described in the Book of Esther. The fourth time, Bar Kokhba battles Amalek (the Romans), loses and is killed.[26] Due to the defeat, the pattern for this critical period does not continue—there is no Third Temple at this

Table 5.1 The Rhythm of History

Divine Plan Set-up		1st Opportunity for Conclusion of Plan		2nd Opportunity for Conclusion of Plan		3rd Opportunity for Conclusion of Plan		
End of Preparatory and 1st Critical Period		End of Preparatory and 2nd Critical Period		End of Preparatory and 3rd Critical Period		End of Preparatory and 4th Critical Period		Pattern
2300	Joseph dies 2309	2800		3300		3800		
2310		2810		3310	Jerusalem is conquered	3810		Disruptive Event
2320		2820		3320		3820	2nd Temple is destroyed 3829	
2330	Slavery begins 2332	2830	Conquest begins after Samson fails in 2831	3330	1st Temple is destroyed 3338	3830		
2340		2840		3340		3840		
2350		2850	David born 2854	3350	Ezra born?	3850	Bar Kokhba born?	Birth of Leader
2360	Moses born 2368	2860		3360	Esther born	3860		
2370		2870		3370		3870		
2380		2880	Saul is appointed King 2882; war with Agag (Amalek) fails 2883	3380		3880	Bar Kokhba revolt (Amalek battle) fails 3893	Leader becomes King, Amalek battle
2390		2890	David becomes King 2892	3390	Building of 2nd Temple begins 3391	3890	Judaism is banned 3894	
2400	Moses strikes the Egyptian and flees 2408	2900		3400	Purim (Amalek battle) 3404-6	3900		
2410	Exodus attempted 2418	2910		3410	2nd Temple is completed 3412	3910	Sanhedrin is re-established and works on Oral Torah 3908	Building of Temple and New Revelation
2420		2920	Building of 1st Temple begins 2928	3420	Time of Ezra	3920		
2430		2930	1st Temple completed 2935	3430		3930		
2440	Moses see the burning bush 2447; Exodus from Egypt and Torah is given 2448; Tabernacle is erected 2449	2940		3440	Ezra dies 3448; officially published all 24 books of the Torah	3940	Yehudah HaNasi completed final editing of Mishna 3949	
2460		2960	Solomon dies; kingdom divided 2964	3460		3960		
2480	Moses dies; children of Israel enter land of Israel 2488	2980		3480	Shimon HaTzaddik dies 3488	3980		Death of Leader
2500		3000		3500		4000	Time of the 4th exile	
	Apportionment of Israel completed 2503				Torah is translated into Greek 3515			

51

point. It is interesting to note that the key religious sage of the time, Rabbi Akiva,[1] suggested that Bar Kokhba[2] might be the Messiah, but he realized this was a mistake after Bar Kokhba was killed.

Building of Temple and New Revelation. Next we have a period of a new beginning. This is marked by the building of the Tabernacle and Temples (except after Bar Kokhba is killed), and by the revelation/dissemination of God's wisdom. Revelation, in particular, occurs on time (i.e., during corresponding years ending in 48/49): the giving of the 10 Commandments and the Torah in 2448 and the second Tablets in 2449, the publication by Ezra of all 24 books of the Torah for the first time in 3448, and the completion by Rabbi Yehudah HaNasi of the key portion of the Oral tradition, the Mishna, in 3949.

Death of Leader. Then we have a period when the leaders and righteous people die, and there is a transition. After Moses dies, the Nation enters the land of Israel; after Solomon dies, the Nation is divided; after Ezra dies, the land of Israel is caught between warring states and is dominated by one or the other; and after the Bar Kokhba revolt fails and he dies, there is the final dispersion of the fourth and current exile.[3]

We can see that history does indeed match the underlying design pattern. Exact dates vary, depending on the behavior of the people at the time. In-depth analysis can shed light on some of the variations, and more events can be added that reinforce the picture, but the pattern is evident.

In Chapter 8 we will extend this pattern into the future to 'predict' the events in the End of Days and compare them to the prophecies of the future discussed in Chapter 3. First, however, we will examine the current preparatory period, corresponding to the time before the End of Days.

Chapter 6

Looking at Recent History

After the destruction of the Second Temple came the fourth exile of Israel, which has lasted almost 2,000 years and will continue until all the Jewish people have returned to Israel. Before the fifth and final critical period, the End of Days, we expect a preparatory period. This period spans the biblical years from 5667 to 5833, or 1907 to 2073 CE (see Table 4.1). The meaning and importance of the exact events during this preparatory period are hard to discern from the prophecies summarized in Chapter 3, but we will make some significant headway by comparing them to the events of prior preparatory periods.

Preparing for the End of Days

In this section, we will put the events of the preparatory period for the Divine Plan set-up—the first preparatory period, 2167–2333, when Jacob and Joseph were preparing the way for the formation of the Israelite nation and the giving of the law—side by side with the events of this current, parallel preparatory period for the Divine Plan conclusion. Surveying the events for these two periods will put everything in perspective, enabling us to understand what has been happening and how far along we are towards the End of Days.

Table 6.1 presents in its second and third columns the events and times for the two preparatory periods; the first column shows the common theme in each instance. Note that the two major themes in that column are: (i) the Jacob and Esau conflict and (ii) the preparation for the establishment of Israel. We will now look at both of these in turn.

Table 6.1 The Preparatory Periods

Theme	Preparatory Period for the Divine Plan Set-up	Preparatory Period for the Conclusion of the Divine Plan
Jacob and Esau Conflict		
Conflict starts	Jacob receives Esau's blessing 2171; Jacob begins his personal exile	Turko Italian War 5671 (1911 CE) which leads to WW1 starting in 5674 (1914 CE)
	Jacob's ladder dream 2185	
	Joseph is born 2199	Hitler's plan of genocide 5699 (1939 CE)
Uneasy peace in the conflict	Jacob and Esau resolve their conflict 2205	WW2 ends 5705 (1945 CE)
Preparation for the Establishment of Israel		
Birth of Israel	Benjamin is born 2208	State of Israel born 5708 (1948 CE)
Struggle with Egypt	Joseph is sold into slavery in Egypt 2216	War with Egypt 5716 (1956 CE) and Iraq / Yemenite Jews immigrate to Israel
Israel's future survival is ensured	Joseph is appointed Viceroy 2229 / should have happened in 2227	Jerusalem comes under Israel rule 5727 (1967 CE War);
Famine and wars	the famine begins 2235	Yom Kippur War 5734 (1973 CE)
Peace with Egypt	Jacob goes to Egypt 2238	Peace with Egypt - Sadat visit 5737 (1977 CE), peace treaty signed 5739 (1979 CE)
Start of the Ishmael-related conflicts and conclusion of the Esau conflicts	Jacob dies 2255	
	Sons of Ishmael and Esau come to wage war	Gulf War 5750-5751 (1990-1991 CE)
	Esau is killed at Jacob's funeral	End of Cold War 5751 (1991 CE)
		USSR dissolved 5752 (1992 CE)
Peace post-Jacob's death	Relative peace in Israel and state building	Ethiopian Jews rescued 5751 (1991 CE)
		Russian Jews rescued 5752 (1992 CE)
		Peace agreement signed between Israel and Jordan 5755 (1994 CE)
		Israel withdraws from Lebanon 5760 (2000 CE)
Ishamel conflicts continue	Descent into slavery	9/11 attack 5761 (2001 CE)
		War in Afghanistan 5762 (2001 CE) to present day
		Iraq war 5763-5771 (2003-2011 CE)
		Unilateral evacuation of 25 Jewish settlements completed 5765 (2005 CE)
		Syrian nuclear reactor destroyed 5767 (2007 CE)
		Israel launched a military operation against Hamas 5773 (2012 CE)
	Joseph dies 2309 - descent into slavery intensifies	??? Circa 5809 (2049 CE)
	Jacob's last surviving son (Levi) dies and slavery begins 2332	??? Circa 5832 (2072 CE)
	1st critical period starts 2332	5th critical period (End of Days) starts

Note: the underlined numbers are to aid in comparing the years shown in the 2nd and 3rd columns.

The Jacob and Esau Conflict

We examined the background of the Jacob and Esau conflict in Chapter 2 and saw that Amalek (Esau's descendant, originally his grandson) would attack to instill doubt in the nation of Israel whenever the Divine Purpose was close at hand. Indeed, in Chapter 5, when we looked back in history, we saw various instances of Amalek's attacks. Beyond the repeating wars with Amalek during the formative period of Israel, we saw the original direct conflict between Jacob and Esau play out.[1] Scripture[2] also foretells a future war—against Gog and Magog—in the End of Days.

So has this original conflict just repeated itself in preparation for the End of Days? Let's take a closer look.

The brothers' conflict is evident in the womb[3] but officially starts when Jacob obtains Isaac's blessing in 2171.[4] Fleeing the anger of Esau, who had expected to receive their father's blessing, Jacob ends up in exile for the next 36 years.[5] Jacob and Esau then reach an uneasy peace, ending the conflict between them but not the general conflict between Amalek and Israel—the Edom conflict.[6]

Table 6.1 shows that the beginning of the conflict between Jacob and Esau in 2171 coincides with the Turko-Italian war of 5671 (1911 CE), the key event that led to the start of World War I three years later. The main conflict between Jacob and Esau ended in 2205, which coincides with the end of World War II in 5705 (1945 CE).

Thus, the conflict between Jacob and Esau parallels the period of the two world wars, which culminated in the genocide of approximately six million Jews and millions of other innocent people during World War II in a program of systematic, state-sponsored murder by Nazi Germany. Even the 'suicidal' behavior of Amalek is exemplified by the actions of Nazi Germany. Consider the following example. With the invasion of Hungary in 1944 CE, top German military officers determined that railway lines had to be prioritized to transport vital troops and equipment to the battlefront. They urged

Hitler to provide this infusion of desperately needed supplies. Instead, ignoring their warnings, Hitler ordered that the precious rail lines be used to deport hundreds of thousands of Hungarian Jews to the extermination camps. Historians identify this decision as a key factor in further debilitating the German war effort. It seems Hitler regarded the Holocaust as more important than winning World War II,[7] and in so doing he behaved like Amalek.

When Kaiser Wilhelm of Germany visited Jerusalem during his journey to the Holy Land in 1898 CE, almost all the religious leaders of Jerusalem came to the city gates to greet him. Rabbi Yosef Chaim Sonnenfeld, at that time the spiritual leader of Ashkenazic[8] Jewry in Israel, did not attend. When asked about his refusal to greet the Kaiser, he answered that he held with the tradition that Germany is a descendent of Amalek.[9]

Preparation for the Establishment of Israel

In the context of the End of Days, the establishment of Israel means the formation of a theocratic state where the Torah law is observed; as such, the process is still ongoing. In the time of Jacob and Joseph, preparation for the giving of the law and for entering Israel as a nation involved Jacob fathering and bringing up 12 sons who would lead the 12 Tribes,[10] and Joseph 'arranging' for the whole family to relocate to Egypt in order to survive the years of famine, and then grow into a people ready for Moses to redeem.[11]

Let's follow the events of Jacob's and Joseph's time, and the parallel events that have occurred in the recent past. You may find it helpful to refer to Table 6.1 along the way.

Birth of Israel. After Jacob and Esau's conflict is resolved, Jacob's twelfth son, Benjamin, is born in 2208. With his birth, all 12 Tribes of Israel are now manifested. That year corresponds to the 'birth' of the state of Israel in 5708 (1948 CE).

Struggle with Egypt. Soon after, in 2216, Joseph is sold into slavery in Egypt. This marks the beginning of the struggle to create a place for the tribes to survive in Egypt. This event corresponds to 5716 (1956 CE), the beginning of the modern struggle with Egypt— the 1956 CE Egypt–Israel war.

Israel's future survival is ensured. Thirteen years later, Joseph is named Viceroy (second-in-command) of Egypt, which ensures that the tribes of Israel will survive. We are told that Joseph's appointment should have taken place two years earlier, in 2227. This time corresponds to 5727 (1967 CE), the year Jerusalem came under Israeli rule, a key step in putting Israel back together.

Famine and Wars. Joseph prepares for the years of famine. In the corresponding period in our recent past, Israel continued to fight wars and prepare for future conflicts.

Peace with Egypt. The famine forces Jacob to come to Egypt with his family in 2238. On arrival, Jacob meets the Pharaoh and is assured of a place for his family to live and thrive. This time corresponds to 5738 (1978 CE), when Israel worked on lasting peace with Egypt, thus cementing its survival by preventing Egypt from joining future wars against Israel. Interestingly, in the 20th century it was the ruler of Egypt, Anwar el-Sadat, who came to Israel to make peace.

Start of the Ishmael-Related Conflicts and Conclusion of the Esau Conflicts. Jacob dies in 2255 after blessing all the tribes. As Jacob's family takes his body from Egypt to Canaan for burial,[12] the sons of Esau and Ishmael come to wage war with them. Ishmael is the ancestor of the Arabic nations, and we will learn more about him later in this chapter.[13] The war is averted, but Esau is killed by one of Jacob's sons or grandsons.[14] His death corresponds to the final closure of the world wars, with the fall of the Berlin Wall and the end of the Cold War. The hostility from Ishmael is also the start of the new set of wars between the West and certain nations and factions in the Middle East, which was prophesied: *"And the children of Ishmael are destined to evoke great wars in the world, and the children of Edom will gather over them and they will wage war with them."*[15] I will elaborate on this whole topic later, in the section on 'Recent Wars.' During this time, additional 'tribes' return to Israel—as seen in the massive Russian and Ethiopian immigrations.

Relative Peace. Following Jacob's death, his family experiences relative peace, which mirrors Israel's current struggle toward peace—its withdrawal from Lebanon, evacuation from settlements, and proactive attacks on Syria and Hamas from 2000 CE until the recent past—and the historically low level of anti-Semitism in the world.

Ishmael Conflicts Continue. There is more conflict as the End of Days approaches.

The 1st preparatory period ends with the death of Jacob's last surviving son, Levi, in 2332; this corresponds to 5832 (2072 CE). Slavery then begins, in a gradual way.[16] As we have seen, the beginning of slavery corresponds to the recurring beginning of disruptive events that precede the critical periods shown in Table 5.1. This future harmful period is described in the prophecies as a time of great calamities.[17]

Hence, the period after Jacob's death and before slavery (corresponding to 1995 through 2072 CE in the current preparatory period) isn't just about relative peace; it's about a gradual descent into slavery. The sources indicate that when Jacob died, "the eyes and heart of Israel were closed because of the suffering of the enslavement, for [the Egyptians] began to enslave them."[18] We have seen that forced enslavement began after Levi's death, not when Jacob died. What the sources mean by "began to enslave them", is that enslavement was an incremental process. Over time, privileges were taken away. Initially, work was intermittent and paid, to get people used to working; later, Pharaoh set an example by working side-by-side with the Israelites, thereby cajoling them to work for free. Eventually, they were fully enslaved.[19]

A key milestone in the enslavement process was Joseph's death (a time equivalent to 2049 CE), when the situation deteriorated significantly. Joseph was Viceroy for 80 years, until the day of his death. He knew that once he died and was no longer the second-in-command, the Egyptians would behave differently towards the Israelites. In fact, Joseph, unlike his father Jacob, did not ask to be taken to Israel for burial at that time but for his body to remain in Egypt and be taken to Israel much later, during the Exodus.[20] Joseph knew that his children, brothers, and their families either would not be allowed to leave Egypt for the burial or would have their possessions pillaged during their absence; with Joseph no longer Viceroy, the Egyptians would fear no retribution.[21] This indicates how far things had deteriorated for the Israelites and how much their freedom was restricted after Joseph's death.

During this descent into slavery, the threat to the Israelites was not just from the Egyptians but also from within. While the Bible prohibits the Israelites from assimilating,[22] this is exactly what occurred. What does "the eyes and heart of Israel were closed" mean? The sages teach that the eyes and heart are the two agents that lead to sin: the eyes to immorality and the heart to idolatry.[23] Thus, after Jacob's death the Israelites begun to assimilate into Egyptian culture, which appealed to their eyes and heart.[24] This assimilation process was slow and steady and involved all Israelites except for the tribe of Levi.

We can see that this period is paralleled in our time; it began in 1995 and will continue through 2049 until 2072 CE.[25] Both periods witnessed a struggle against Edom and the building of Israel in preparation for the subsequent critical period. We also see that the near future, as we approach 2049 CE and beyond (to 2072), will include loss of freedom and assimilation into modern culture, leading to the "period of great calamities" that precedes the End of Days.

Messiah ben Joseph

Is the current period, which we have been experiencing since the early 1900s CE, the period of building and preparation for the coming of Messiah ben David that the prophecy says will occur under the leadership of Messiah ben Joseph? After all, the key events in putting Israel back together and returning many of the exiles have been decisively military and political in nature—the main function of Messiah ben Joseph. If so, can we identify Messiah ben Joseph? At this point, probably not.

Recent Wars

In the historical overview presented in Chapter 5, we observed a pattern of recurring battles with Amalek. In our recent past, reviewed earlier in this chapter, we identified the two world wars as potentially part of that pattern of recurring battles. Looking forward, as we shall see in Chapter 8, the prophecies and the pattern of biblical history predict a final battle, the war of Gog and Magog, in which Amalek is to be eradicated.

However, other significant battles have been and are still raging in our recent past and present time, many related to the establishment of Israel or in Israel's environs. These battles are with Israel's neighbors, and although many have involved Israel, some (e.g., the Gulf War, the 9/11 attacks, the war in Afghanistan, and the Iraq War, shown in Table 6.1) have involved other Western countries.

Is there more to the war of Gog and Magog than we have discussed? Yes. The subject is shrouded in mystery and thus will not be definitively clear until the End of Days. However, we can examine some of the sources and see whether they shed light on recent events. Before we can examine this coming war, though, we need some background on Ishmael, a significant biblical figure whose descendants will play a key role in the war of Gog and Magog.

Ishmael

In this section it is useful to refer to the Figure 2.1 showing Abraham's Family tree, and the further elaboration of the Ishmael and Esau relationship depicted in Figure 6.1.

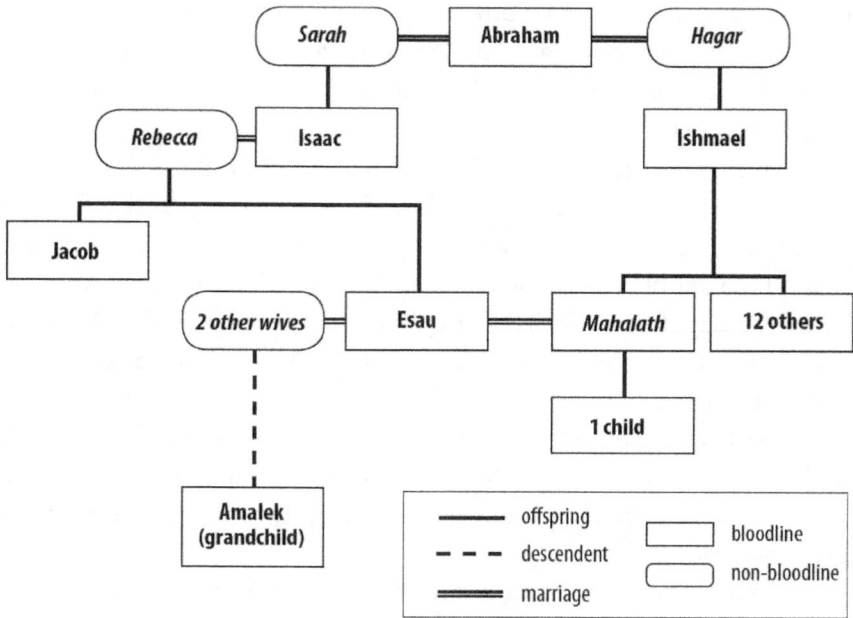

Figure 6.1 The Ishmael and Esau relationship

Abraham begot Isaac, who begot Jacob and Esau. Esau then became the progenitor of the nation of Edom (including Amalek).[26] Abraham's wife Sarah, thinking she was barren, gave her maid Hagar to Abraham,[27] and they had Ishmael (biblical year 2035, or 1727 BCE), 13 years before Sarah and Abraham had Isaac.

An angel of God declared Ishmael *"a wild-ass of a man; his hand against everyone, and everyone's hand against him and over his brother shall he dwell."*[28] The commentaries interpret this to mean that Ishmael was destined to be a plunderer and warrior, dependent on other nations who, in turn, would depend on him.[29] *His hand against everyone* meant that at first his progeny would be victorious against all people; but *everyone's hand against him* indicated that ultimately, they would conquer him. Furthermore, a key commentary relates that since Sarah *"dealt harshly with"*[30] Hagar, Ishmael's descendants would afflict Sarah's descendants (Israel and Edom).[31] Note that this prophecy seems very accurate in our day, as the Arab nations depend on Western technology, while the West depends on their oil, and conflicts are erupting at many levels.

Sarah, concerned about the influence Ishmael might have on Isaac, asked Abraham to send Ishmael away.[32] Despite the fact that Abraham discerned many positive qualities in his son and wanted to make Ishmael his heir, God insisted that his covenant with Abraham be perpetuated specifically through Isaac and Isaac's descendants[33] and that Abraham grant Sarah's request.[34] Thus, Abraham sent Hagar and Ishmael away with water and food.

Hagar and Ishmael lost their way in the wilderness of Beer Sheba and soon ran out of water,[35] but an angel appeared and assured Hagar that they would be saved and that Ishmael would be the father of a great nation.[36]

Ishmael grew up into a strong man, living on the outskirts of the desert and becoming a great archer. He married and had many children, who multiplied and became known as Ishmaelites, or Arabs, the people of the desert.[37] Later in life, Ishmael repented for his prior misdeeds before dying at the age of 137.[38] Ishmael is recognized as an important prophet, a Patriarch of Islam, and the ancestor of several prominent Arab tribes.

Is there more to the family relationship between Esau and Ishmael than we have seen thus far? Yes.

When Esau was 40, he married two women, both from the Canaanite tribe of the Hittites. Isaac and his wife were bitter about these non-Abrahamic wives.[39] Later, Esau also married Mahalath, a daughter of Ishmael and thus a granddaughter of Abraham.[40]

Thus emerges the further relationship between the descendants of Esau and Ishmael (although Amalek himself came from a different wife than Ishmael's daughter).

Gog and Magog Revisited

In Chapter 3, we learned the following about the war of Gog and Magog: (i) it will be a climactic battle in the early stages of the Messianic Era; (ii) Gog and Magog, the forces of evil, will undertake to battle not only Israel but the Almighty Himself; (iii) Magog refers to a place, land, nation, or alliance of nations; (iv) Magog will be led by a king, Gog; (v) the identities of Gog and Magog are unknown.

Although we do not know who Magog and Gog are today, they must include some of Esau's descendants, as in this final war, Amalek will be eradicated. We also have other hints that it involves the descendants of Ishmael.

One is that the prophet Ezekiel[41] identifies the nations involved as Persia, Cush, Put, Meshech, and Tuval. Edom—which is associated with Meshech and Tuval—is on the list, as we would expect. But so are peoples associated with Ishmael and his descendants: Persia = Iran, Cush = portions of Egypt and Sudan, and Put = parts of Libya.[42] Thus, it appears that descendants of Esau and Ishmael will join forces against the descendants of Jacob.

This concept of Esau and Ishmael planning to join forces against Jacob is also part of the deeper meaning behind Esau marrying Mahalath, a daughter of Ishmael. Esau and Ishmael's intentions in uniting their forces were not solely for mutual benefit. Each desired to eventually wipe out the other and seize total power in the world.[43]

Another hint is that the book of Daniel[44] refers to the union of Edom and Ishmael in the End of Days. Nebuchadnezzar, King of Babylon, has a dream in which he sees a huge statue with a head of gold, an upper torso of silver, belly and thighs of copper, legs of iron, and feet partially of iron and partially of earthenware. Daniel reveals that each part of the statue represents a different sovereign kingdom that will wield power in the world. The order progresses downward from the head to the feet, with the parts representing Babylon, Persia,

Greece, and Rome.[45] The iron portion of the feet are usually interpreted to be Edom and the earthenware component to be Ishmael or different factions of Ishmael.[46] Daniel predicts that the two kingdoms of Edom and Ishmael will be in a power struggle until the final war of Gog and Magog.[47]

Is there one war of Gog and Magog or many? There are hints of many. If so, when do they occur?

Some say to expect three wars. According to the Malbim (1809–79 CE), a great biblical commentator,[48] in the first battle, the armies of Gog and Magog will be defeated just as they enter the borders of the Land of Israel. In the second battle, they will penetrate the Land of Israel but will be defeated before they can attack Jerusalem. The final encounter will be a siege upon Jerusalem itself, ultimately thwarted. Some have speculated that the first two battles correspond to the two world wars.

Similarly, the Talmud[49] refers to *"the wars of Gog and Magog,"* plural. Some interpret this to mean they are actually divided into many wars and travails throughout the period leading up to the final Redemption (in the preparatory period and the End of Days).[50]

Finally, the mystical tradition contains the following prophecies:

> *The children of Ishmael will cause great wars [plural] in the world and the children of Edom will gather against them and wage war against them, one on the sea, one on the dry land, and one near Jerusalem. And each one will prevail over the other, but the Holy Land will not be given over to the children of Edom.51*

> *And the sons of Ishmael will go up at that time [the End of Days] to arouse all the nations of the world to come upon Jerusalem, as it says "And I will gather all of the nations to Jerusalem for war" (Zechariah 14:2), and it is written "And the kings of the earth will gather and the rulers will take counsel on God and his Messiah" (Psalms 2:2).52*

All sources agree the wars are during *"the final years."* Most equate these final years to the End of Days, but some notable commentaries say the final years also include the period of preparation for the End of Days.[53]

If the main participants in the war of Gog and Magog will be Edom's descendants, Ishmael's descendants, and Israel, what about the people of the Far East (China, the rest of Asia, etc.)? What is their role? So far we have spoken about Abraham's first two wives and children. After Sarah's death, Abraham married Keturah (whom some commentaries say was Hagar[54]). He fathered six children with her, then:

> *Abraham gave all he had to Isaac. But to the concubine-children who were Abrahams [and Keturah's], Abraham gave gifts,[55] then he sent them away from Isaac his son, while he was still alive, eastward to the land of the east.[56]*

How far east did Abraham send them? *"He counselled them: the farther you can go to the rising of the sun, go, lest you be burnt by the burning coal of Isaac."*[57] Thus, these children were sent to the Far East to have a destiny divorced from Israel (which history has proven), and they will remain separate, not playing a role in the war of Gog and Magog. In the Far East, these children developed a world of spiritual potential—higher than in the West—based on Abraham's "gifts"[58] of wisdom.

Given all of the above—what's going on?

It's not clear, but what we can discern is that many nations are involved in wars, and the earlier battles can be correlated to recent wars between the West and Afghanistan/Iraq, as well as to the Middle East wars. Nonetheless, the final war of Gog and Magog has not occurred because its outcome has not yet happened, and because prophecy and extrapolation from historical events place it in the future—as we shall see in Chapter 8. In the book of Ezekiel, God addresses Gog to tell us that through the war of Gog and Magog, the nations will come to recognize God's unique plan for the world:

> *It will be at the End of Days that I will bring you upon My land, in order that the nations will know Me, when I become sanctified through you before their eyes, O Gog!*[59]

Perhaps the stage is now set. The State of Israel is back, albeit not yet completely as envisioned in the End of Days prophecy. Dispersed Jews from many parts of the world have returned to Israel, although more than half remain outside, mostly in the United States.[60] Numerous kinds of conflicts are occurring. If all these events are indeed a preparation for the coming of the Messiah, then right now we are in a relatively quiet time, before a period of great calamities that will usher in the End of Days.

Chapter 7

Disclaimer

The goal of a disclaimer is to make sure people are aware they are reading information at their own risk. The opinions being provided are for information only and are not intended to be used in planning your life. (Or are they?)

The sources are clear: no one can know the exact form of future events, or their timing.[1] Most importantly, can we change the future and take a shortcut by bringing the Messiah sooner?[2] Yes. As discussed in Chapter 3, if we are worthy—"*I* [God] *will hasten it.*"[3]

We have already seen that we can usher in the era of universal peace by humankind at large observing the Seven Noahide Laws and by Jews observing the 613 commandments of the Torah. Thus, far from being an event out of our control, the time of the arrival of the Messiah is in our hands, but it depends on our collective merit. Every individual can bring the Messianic era closer by improving his actions, his character, and by inspiring others to do the same.

The sources indicate a number of ways of hastening the Messianic Era. These involve the observance of certain comprehensive principles of the law.[4] For example:

Submission to God and His will: the sincere thought of regretting misdeeds with a determination to better our ways and become more holy.[5]

> *When you return unto God, your God, and will listen to His voice... God, your God, will return your captivity and have compassion upon you, and He will restore and gather you from all the nations to which God, your God, has dispersed you...*[6]

Observance of the Sabbath,[7] expressing the recognition and belief that God created the world.

> *If Israel were to keep two Sabbaths according to the laws thereof, they would be redeemed immediately.*[8]

Compassion for the needy and downcast, evoking a reciprocal compassion from Heaven.[9]

> *Maintain justice and do what is right, for my [God's] salvation is close at hand and my righteousness will soon be revealed.*[10]

Performing one good deed, at the right time, that someone else cannot perform. Throughout the year, a person should view himself and his relationship to the entire world as if his good and bad deeds are evenly balanced. By performing one sin, he tips his own scale and that of the entire world to the side of guilt, bringing punishment upon himself and the whole world. Conversely, if he performs one good deed, he tips his scale and that of the entire world to the side of merit, bringing redemption and deliverance to himself and others. As it is written, *"A righteous man is the foundation of the world"* (Proverbs 10:25), meaning that a person who acts virtuously tips the scale of the entire world to the side of merit and saves it.[11]

But what if we don't hasten the coming of the Messiah? The End of Days will still happen by default—it's guaranteed to happen—and the default time when it will happen is predetermined (see Chapter 3).

With this guarantee in mind, Chapter 8 aims only at extending the pattern and trend of history established in Chapter 5, and comparing that extension to the prophecies about the future. This extension of the pattern and trend of history into the future is perhaps the default scenario that we can expect for the End of Days. As we ponder this default scenario, some of its upcoming difficult parts, and how far into the future universal peace lies, we can continuously think about *"hastening"* the End of Days.

Chapter 8

Looking Forward—The End of Days

In Chapter 5, we examined four parallel critical periods of history. The first was a Divine Plan set-up period; the other three could each have led to the End of Days but did not. A clear pattern of events and their approximate default timing emerged.

In this chapter, we look at the fifth and final parallel critical period and the time beyond it.

The Final Critical Period

From the pattern that has emerged based on the four previous critical periods, we can extrapolate and forecast the events and timing of this fifth critical period. We can also examine the prophecies of the future in light of this pattern and glimpse what may be the default scenario and timing for the End of Days.

Table 8.1 is the same as Table 5.1 but with the future fifth critical period added, including a final column displaying the equivalent time in Gregorian calendar years for this period.

Table 8.1 Looking Forward

Divine Plan Set-up	1st Opportunity for Conclusion of Plan	2nd Opportunity for Conclusion of Plan	3rd Opportunity for Conclusion of Plan	Conclusion of Divine Plan (forecast)	
End of Preparatory and 1st Critical Period	End of Preparatory and 2nd Critical Period	End of Preparatory and 3rd Critical Period	End of Preparatory and 4th Critical Period	End of Preparatory and 5th Critical Period	CE year
2300 Joseph dies 2309	2800	3300	3800	5800 Bad times begin	2040
2310	2810	3310 Jerusalem is conquered	3810	5810 Bad times begin	2050
2320	2820	3320	3820 2nd Temple is destroyed 3829	5820	2060
2330 Slavery begins 2332	2830 Conquest begins after Samson fails in 2831	3330 1st Temple is destroyed 3338	3830	5830	2070
2340	2840	3340	3840	5840	2080
2350	2850 David born 2854	3350 Ezra born?	3850 Bar Kokhba born?	5850 Messiah is born	2090
2360 Moses born 2368	2860	3360 Esther born	3860	5860	2100
2370	2870	3370	3870	5870	2110
2380	2880 Saul is appointed King 2882; war with Agog (Amalek) fails 2881	3380	3880 Bar Kokhba revolt (Amalek battle) fails 3893	5880 Messiah becomes King	2120
2390	2890 David becomes King 2892	3390 Building of 2nd Temple begins 3391	3890 Judaism is banned 3894	5890 Gog and Magog War	2130
2400 Moses strikes the Egyptian and flees 2408	2900	3400 Purim (Amalek battle) 3404-6	3900	5900	2140
2410 Exodus attempted 2418	2910	3410 2nd Temple is completed 3412	3910 Sanhedrin is re-established and works on Oral Torah 3908	5910 3rd Temple is built	2150
2420	2920 Building of 1st Temple begins 2928	3420 Time of Ezra	3920	5920	2160
2430	2930 1st Temple completed 2935	3430	3930	5930	2170
2440 Moses see the burning bush 2447; Exodus from Egypt and Torah is given 2448; Tabernacle is erected 2449	2940	3440 Ezra dies 3448; officially published all 24 books of the Torah	3940 Yehudah HaNasi completed final editing of Mishna 3949	5940 Inner Torah is revealed	2180
2460	2960 Solomon dies; kingdom divided 2964	3460	3960	5960	2200
2480 Moses dies; children of Israel enter land of Israel 2488	2980	3480 Shimon HaTzaddik dies 3488	3980	5980 Resurrection of the dead	2220
2500	3000	3500	4000 Time of the 4th exile	6000	2240
Apportionment of Israel completed 2503		Torah is translated into Greek 3515		7th millenium	

70

In Table 8.1, the events in the future are a forecast based on the pattern of the prior four periods (see the Pattern column in Table 5.1). As you can see, forecasting is not hard. The events will proceed as follows.

Bad times begin

Following the death of Joseph (and Messiah ben Joseph), a bad period will begin circa 2050 CE and might last into the critical period. In the past, this was marked by conquest, the destruction of the Temples, and exile. The prophecy says it will be a period of great calamities.[1]

Messiah is born and becomes King

The Messiah (ben David) will be born circa 2090 and become King circa 2120 CE. This corresponds to the time of King David and Solomon, the first redeemer (Moses),[2] and other significant leaders such as Ezra and Bar Kokhba.

Gog and Magog War

The onset of the Messianic Era will soon be challenged by the renewed battle with Amalek circa 2130 CE. This time it will be the final prophesied Gog and Magog War, coinciding with the times of prior wars with Amalek.

Third Temple is built

Once Amalek has been overcome forever, the third and final Temple will be built circa 2150 CE; this period coincides with the completion of the prior two Temples.

Inner Torah is revealed

After the building of the Third Temple will be this next major revelation, circa 2188 CE. This coincides with past revelations: the original Sinai revelation, the publishing of the 24 books of the written Torah, and the compilation of the oral Torah. The mystical Torah will in no way be 'new' in terms of instruction; the newness will be in our understanding and comprehension of the inner or hidden meaning of the existing Torah.[3] This process began slowly, on time, at the start of this final cycle of history, in the early 5500s (circa 1740 CE), with the Ba'al Shem Tov (Rabbi Yisrael ben Eliezer),[4] and will reach a new height and dissemination with the coming of the Messiah.[5]

Resurrection of the Dead

Next will be the prophesied resurrection of the dead, circa 2220 CE. We explored this earlier, in Chapter 3. This event coincides with the righteous people of prior critical periods dying in this time frame; notably, however, the righteous people are the exception and will be resurrected earlier than others, immediately upon the Messiah's arrival.[6] The process will proceed in two steps: the body will be resurrected, and the soul will be reunited with the body. There are different opinions as to how the physical process of resurrection will take place: either a new body will grow organically or bones will rise and recover their flesh. The physical resurrection may happen anywhere in the world, but the actual restoration of the soul to the body will only take place in the Land of Israel.[7]

Seventh Millennium

Finally, there is a transition to the seventh millennium by 2240 CE, coinciding with past positive (entering Israel) and negative (division of the nation and exile) transitions.

As we saw in Chapter 3, the exact meaning and order of events is not completely clear from Scripture. However, the pattern revealed by history clearly shows the overall sequence and general timing of events. This pattern does not provide information on the completed return to Israel of the exiled and lost tribes. As we saw, much of this return has been taking place in this preparatory period. However, the process is as yet incomplete. One understanding from the sources is that the ingathering of the exiles will be completed after the Third Temple stands and 40 years before the resurrection of the dead.[8] Based upon the observations summarized in Table 8.1, the completion of the ingathering will occur circa 2180 CE, around the time of the revelation of the inner Torah.

Further Clarifying the Picture

With the aid of the overall design of history and an examination of past critical periods, we have developed a picture of the fifth critical period. But the past historical events that we have used to glimpse into the future are not our only tools. Adam's activities on Day 6 and the Hebrew alphabet can both help us explore the future.

The Timeline of Adam's Sin and How It Helps Us Forecast

> The end is enwedged in the beginning, and the beginning in the end.[9]

The pattern and timing of Adam's activities at the end of Creation Day 6 correspond to our present time and our future, and they also shed light on the end of the sixth millennium, at the End of Days. Let's consider this possibility further.

Adam was created on Day 6, starting at daybreak. Each Creation day is a long period of time but is nonetheless divided into 24 'hours.' The day starts in the evening (nominally 6 p.m.), then proceeds through 12 hours of darkness (to 6 a.m.) and 12 hours of daylight (to 6 p.m.); the hours of daylight are described as hours one through 12.

The Babylonian Talmud describes in detail the activities related to Adam during the 12 hours of daylight:

> *In the first hour, his [Adam's] dust was gathered; in the second, it was kneaded into a shapeless mass. In the third, his limbs were shaped; in the fourth, a soul was infused into him; in the fifth, he arose and stood on his feet; in the sixth, he gave [the animals] their names; in the seventh, Eve became his mate; in the eighth, they ascended to bed as two and descended as four [i.e., Cain and Abel were born]; in the ninth, he was commanded not to eat of the tree; in the tenth, he sinned; in the eleventh, he was tried; and in the twelfth, he was expelled [from Eden] and departed, for it is written, Man abideth not in honor.*[10]

The sequence of events related to Adam can be grouped into three sets of exactly four hours each. Hours 1–4 are devoted to designing Adam's body; this is akin to the right-hand sefirah: kindness or giving. Hours 5–8 are spent limiting and shaping him. He is given an infinite soul, but it is placed in his finite body. He gets split in two—Adam and Eve—and then has descendants (who won't get along). This is all related to the left-hand sefirah: severity or constraining. Hours 9–12 are devoted to testing Adam and thus are a critical period.

Since Day 6 corresponds to the sixth millennium, the final 12 hours of Day 6 correspond to the last 500 years of the millennium— years 5501 to 6000 (1741 to 2240 CE). Table 8.2 shows how the events of the last five hours (the first being at the end of the preparatory period and the last four corresponding to the critical period) of Day 6 match the events for the equivalent years we discussed earlier in this chapter (see Table 8.1). Recall that in this equivalent period we are to undo or finally correct Adam's sin. Thus, we would expect that we will do the opposite of what Adam did— e.g., where he sinned, we are not going to. Right?

The first column in Table 8.2 shows the key events, with their biblical year, for the conclusion of the Divine Plan, the End of Days; we determined these in the previous section (in Table 8.1, see the column labeled Conclusion of Divine Plan). The next column shows the equivalent Gregorian calendar year. The third column shows the equivalent hour in Day 6, and the final column shows Adam's action during this hour.

Table 8.2 Adam's Sin vs. the End of Days

Conclusion of Divine Plan (forecast)		CE Year	Day 6 Timing	Event
5800		2040		
5810	Bad times begin	2050	Hour 8	Adam bears children
5820		2060		
5830		2070		
5840		2080		
5850	Messiah is born	2090	Hour 9	Adam is commanded
5860		2100		
5870		2110		
5880	Messiah becomes King	2120		
5890	Gog and Magog War	2130	Hour 10	Adam sins
5900		2140		
5910	3rd Temple is built	2150		
5920		2160		
5930		2170	Hour 11	Adam is judged
5940	Inner Torah is revealed	2180		
5950		2190		
5960		2200		
5970		2210	Hour 12	Human death instituted
5980	Resurrection of the dead	2220		
5990		2230		
6000	7th millennium	2240		Adam is exiled from Eden

Referring to Table 8.2, we see several correspondences:

Hour 8. Adam consummates his marriage and has children. This corresponds to the beginning of the bad times. Why? Because Adam was not supposed to consummate his marriage until the end of Day 6.[11] Not only did he jump the gun, but he did so in view of the animals, including the snake. This turned out to be the key event that precipitated the sin.[12]

Hour 9. Adam is commanded by God. This corresponds to the time when the Messiah will appear to command humanity.

Hour 10. Adam sins at the beginning of the hour.[13] This corresponds to the time of the Gog and Magog War, the final war with Amalek, and the subsequent building of the Third Temple. Why? The sin began when the snake instilled doubt in Eve; Genesis 3.1–4 contains the dialogue between the snake and Eve. The snake is viewed in the sources as the root of Amalek.[14] Thus, the war with Amalek corresponds to the initial 'war' with the snake, which the snake won by convincing Eve to eat the fruit. After the sin, the Divine Presence was repelled from the Garden. This is the opposite of what we will do to rectify the sin, as we will win the war against Amalek. Then we will build the Third Temple and draw the Divine Presence back.

Hour 11. Adam is judged and therefore must leave the idyllic existence in the Garden and enter our world. This corresponds to our doing the opposite. We are to transition from our current existence and our secular world into an existence very similar to the original one—and a revelation of the Divine Presence—in the Garden. This means an existence in the presence of God, and a time of universal peace, plenty, health, and contentment.

Hour 12. Adam becomes mortal and is expelled from Eden; prior to the sin, Adam was to be immortal, but the sin brought about human death.[15] This corresponds to the resurrection of the dead into eternal life and the transition to the seventh millennium.

So yes, the pattern and timing of Adam's activities at the end of Day 6 do indeed shed light on the end of the sixth millennium, at the End of Days. The events of Day 6 correspond inversely and remarkably accurately to the predictions of events for the End of Days, based on the pattern of history. We will undo Adam's sin.

The Hebrew Letters and How They Help Us Forecast

Five of the 22 letters in the Hebrew alphabet have different forms when positioned at the end of a word versus anywhere else in the word. We call these the five final letters. Do these letters correspond to the five critical periods or potential ends of time? If so, do they reinforce the events of the five critical periods? Yes, and this last section of this chapter explains how.

The universe was created by means of the Hebrew alphabet's 22 letters; as the Genesis narrative frequently tells us, God created via speech: "*and God said . . . .*" As Yitzchak Ginsburgh explains,

> They [the five final letters] allude to five ends, or redemptions from the darkness of our exile within the consciousness of plurality to the light of the final awareness of God's absolute unity. We are taught that the first four ends . . . have already become (partially) manifest in the redemptions of the past. The final end . . . [the fifth letter] awaits the coming of the Mashiach.[16]

Whenever these five final letters are discussed in the Talmud they are always presented in a particular order.[17] In Hebrew, a letter has a meaning derived from its form, numerical value, and association with scripture. Table 8.3 presents the five final letters in order, the meaning of each letter, its association with a historical event, and how the letter corresponds to each critical period or potential 'end' of history.

Table 8.3   The Final Hebrew Letters and the Five Critical Periods

Final Letter[18]	Meaning of the Letter	Association of the Letter[19]	Critical Period to which the Letter Corresponds
Mem (m) מ	Foundation of wisdom	The Torah	**1st Critical Period:** Giving of the Torah
Nun (n) נ	The Messiah, heir to the throne	King David	**2nd Critical Period:** King David and the building of the First Temple
Zadi (z) צ	Faith of the righteous one	Heroes of Purim	**3rd Critical Period:** Purim (a battle won by faith) and the completion of the Second Temple
Pei (p) פ	Communication	The Oral Torah	**4th Critical Period:** Completion of the Mishna
Kaf (k) כ	The power to actualize	The Final Redemption?	**5th Critical Period:** Actualization of the spiritual potential into the physical reality

We can clearly see the correspondence between the five final letters and the potential ends of history or critical periods, as follows:

The **final Mem** refers to wisdom, which is always associated with the Torah. The 1st critical period corresponded to the giving of the Torah.

The **final Nun** is associated with king Messiah, particularly with King David. The 2nd critical period was dominated by King David and the building of the First Temple.

The **final Zadi** is associated with the righteous one. During the 3rd critical period, the battle against Amalek (prior to the completion of the Second Temple) relied on a very righteous leader and the full faith of the people.[20]

The **final Pei** means communication and is always associated with the Oral Torah. The 4th critical period culminated with the completion of the key part of the Oral Torah—the Mishna.

The **final Kaf** is associated with the power of the spiritual realm to fully manifest in the physical realm. This is the purpose of the Messianic Era, the upcoming 5th critical period.

Everything indeed fits the same Divine Plan, as the design of the five critical periods is fundamentally based on and mirrored in the Hebrew alphabet's five final letters.

Chapter 9

The World to Come

<u>Summary of Terms Concerning the Future</u>

End of Days: A time period concerned with the final events in history.

Some religions refer to the End of Days as the Messianic Era.

Messianic Era: An age when, under the leadership of the Messiah, the whole world will believe in one God and live together in peace and brotherhood; expected to start on or before the biblical year 6000, or 2240 CE.

The Messianic Era, or the End of Days, culminates with the Resurrection of the Dead.

Resurrection of the Dead: A future event when the dead will be brought back to life and healed.

The Resurrection of the Dead is followed by life in the World to Come.

World to Come: The time after the End of Days, the seventh millennium being its first stage. Not part of this world.

Now that we have glimpsed the events and timing of the End of Days, we can explore what lies beyond: the seventh millennium. What will it be like to live during the seventh millennium? Will there be life and time beyond the seventh millennium? If not, what will there be?

The biblical chronology consists of three stages or eras, as we explored in Chapter 1 (see Figure 1.1): the 6 Days of Creation, followed by 6,000 years of history, followed by the 1,000 years of the seventh millennium.[1] Adam was created in Day 6, and towards the evening of that day, he sinned and changed the world order. That gave rise to what is referred to as 'this world.'[2] 'This world' proceeds through 6,000 years of history and culminates with the End of Days. We have explored the events and timing for the End of Days. We have also described the prophecies relating to the End of Days—in particular, that we will reach a state of universal peace and, as the last in a series of steps that occur during the End of Days, we will be resurrected from the dead.

The End of Days, despite its lofty description compared to our existence so far, is strictly a part of this world, though it is an intermediary between this world and what comes next. Since it is part of this world, it will occur toward the end of the 6,000 years of history. Once we are resurrected, we will proceed to the World to Come.[3] The first stage in this new era of time is the seventh millennium. But it does not end there—it keeps going.

Let's first recap what has happened in each time period, as this will prepare us to glimpse life in the World to Come. It's important to realize that all direct prophecies about the future relate to the End of Days period. The World to Come is indescribable in our language and thus is not directly described in the prophetic writings; according to the Babylonian Talmud, "*All prophets prophesied only regarding the day of Messiah; regarding the World to Come, 'No eye can behold it. O God, save yours* (Isaiah 64:3).'"[4]

Where we Have Come from: A Quick Review

In order to understand where the Messiah will lead us, we first need to ensure we grasp where we have come from.

We started in an idyllic existence in the Garden of Eden, where the revelation of God was completely evident and the distinction between good and evil was crystal clear. Hence, although there was free will in Eden, it was 'easy' to make the right moral choices. Choosing the wrong thing was like inserting one's hand into fire: the consequences were clear. Nonetheless, Adam and Eve went against their one commandment: not to eat fruit from the Tree of the Knowledge of Good and Evil until the end of Day 6—instead, they ate three hours before the end of the day.[5] Had they obeyed the commandment, Adam and Eve would have given birth to the Messiah[6] and ushered in the World to Come. But they failed to do the right thing during this critical period and as a consequence were expelled from the Garden of Eden,[7] leading to our existence in 'this world.' The sin also brought a mixture of good and evil into the world.[8] Thus, today, choosing what is right is much more complicated and less obvious than it was in the Garden.

As of 2017 CE, we have spent 5777 years in this world. The purpose of our existence here has been to bring both ourselves and the world back to its original state of spiritual sensitivity—or, as we have discussed throughout this book, to create a dwelling place for the Divine Presence in this world. At the end of this period (i.e., the end of this world), during the End of Days, we will be led by the Messiah, who will help us (i) return to the state of clarity originally provided in the Garden of Eden, (ii) complete the correction of Adam and Eve's transgression, and (iii) establish a universal cognizance of God.

As we proceeded from Eden to this world, God instituted death.[9] When a person dies, his body and soul separate. His soul goes to the World of the Souls,[10] and the body is buried in the ground, where it returns to its most elemental form, dust. Later in time, as the last step in the events of the End of Days—the resurrection of the dead—the body is reconstituted.[11] At that point, when we are in a completely new kind of environment, with unprecedented opportunity for earning closeness to God, body and soul will be recombined and the soul will then be able to fully purify the body in preparation for eternal life.

Thus, the Messianic era will be a stepping stone to the World to Come.

Life in the World to Come

Opinions vary both between and within religions as to what life in the World to Come will be like. However, most opinions share similar themes. Here, we will focus on one approach[12] that contains many of the shared themes: body and soul exist together in some altered actuality, enjoying closeness to God in relation to how life was lived in this world, and progressing through a number of stages (starting with the seventh millennium).

In the World to Come that will exist after the resurrection, every soul will finally reach its full potential. After the reversal of Adam's transgression, man's soul will finally accomplish the purpose for which it was created. Each soul will assume full control, purifying the physical body to the maximum extent possible. This will be unlike the situation today, when our bodily desires often drive our actions. Then, both body and soul will continue to grow toward ultimate spirituality, forever enjoying the delight of closeness to God, for which we were created. There will be various stages, starting with the seventh millennium and perhaps eventually culminating in a purely spiritual existence.

It is very difficult to envision the resurrection and the new reality of the World to Come. Fortunately, the butterfly helps us understand the resurrection,[13] and wine helps us understand our future.

Consider the experience of a butterfly, which starts as a caterpillar, a rather ugly, wormlike creature, crawling on a branch. The caterpillar undergoes a metamorphosis and eventually a beautiful butterfly bursts forth and flies gracefully into the air. So too, near the end of our lives, our bodies will be like the wormlike creature—old and worn out, largely concealing our soul, and ready to leave this world. But one day, during the resurrection of the dead, we will emanate in a new, beautiful 'edition,' with a soul fully revealed and shining through the body.[14]

Everything in this world gets worse with time and eventually decays, except good wine, which improves with time. The single most important factor in making a good wine is to pay attention to every detail of the process. This is analogous to living with attention to either the Seven Noahide Laws (for non-Jews) or the 613 commandments of the Torah (for Jews),[15] the details for the process of living. Provided we have worked hard on improving ourselves in these ways, we too can develop ourselves into good 'wine' in this world and enter an existence in the World to Come where we just get better—that is, closer to God. However, if we don't work on improving ourselves very much and consequently develop into mediocre 'wine' in this world, then our existence in the World to Come will be at that lower level—we won't be so close to God. If we don't do any work to improve ourselves in this world, then we might just decay and not be resurrected for the World to Come.

Let's examine life in the World to Come a little more closely now that the analogy of wine has allowed us to understand how self-development will affect our existence there. The post-resurrection World to Come will usher in an entirely new form of existence. The nature of the World to Come flows from its purpose: to provide a venue for experiencing closeness to God. Hence, spirituality and awareness of God will be much more apparent than it is today. The physical world will be altered to facilitate receiving rather than earning closeness to the Divine.[16]

In this world, while we are striving toward improving ourselves, we are placed in a setting to facilitate the process—a setting of challenge and struggle, where the physical and spiritual are in constant strife, where bodily desires and spiritual desires often conflict. In the World to Come, the exact opposite will be the case.

In the Messianic era, which is the stepping stone to the World to Come, we will conquer selfishness and prejudice and will live in a harmonious world community that devotes its energies and resources to the common good, and the quest for continued growth in wisdom and perfection. Thus, the Messianic era will also be a period of improving ourselves and the world, although it will present different challenges from our present day struggles.

Today, our lives involve combating the negative: bringing peace to warring factions, defeating disease, enlightening the ignorant and feeding the hungry. In the Messianic era, when these things have been overcome, we will focus on the attainment of ever greater heights within the realm of good itself. The pursuit of peace will be about finding deeper ways for people to fuse their differences; medicine will concern itself with perfecting health and enhancing the bond between body and soul; and ignorance will be replaced with universal knowledge of God.[17]

It must be understood that the purpose of Creation is not just the completion and perfection of the individual. Rather, it is the bringing of the whole of Creation and the entire history of humankind to a state of holistic completion.[18] As long as some people are performing evil deeds and only some are doing good, there exists a separation between the Divine and this world, and God is therefore not completely revealed here. Thus, we are all dependent on each other to contribute our individual, unique spiritual perfection to a symphony of mankind during the Messianic era, creating the environment that will allow God to dwell here.[19]

In the World to Come, rather than strife, conflict, and challenge prevailing, the soul will triumph, and the body's desires and physical needs will be totally subjugated. Thus, the two worlds are suited for their purpose: this world operates according to laws conducive to man's effort, while the World to Come will function in accordance with laws fit for receiving reward for man's effort made in this world. It will be a deathless existence, overflowing with natural bounty and endless resources, imbued with peace, an altered sense of time, and continual spiritual elevation.[20]

Chapter 10

Conclusion—Where to from Here?

The Messiah, the Anointed One, the Great Peacemaker, and the Ultimate Leader will be a human being, the prophesied descendant of King David, who, thanks to his leadership ability and knowledge of Torah, will inspire the whole world to believe in one God and usher in an era of all human beings living together in peace and brotherhood—the Messianic Era.

When Adam and Eve ate fruit from the Tree of Knowledge of Good and Evil, they created a mixture of good and evil in the world. Ever since, in the long course of history, it has been up to their descendants to clarify the distinction between good and evil. Once this clarification process is complete, the Messiah may be born.[1] But can we use free will to make the right moral choice, or is it all predetermined?

Let's briefly pause now to make sure we address a major theological issue at the crux of what we have been exploring: the intersection of Divine Providence and free will. The two concepts seem completely at odds: either everything is preordained and proceeding according to a plan, or we have complete free will—i.e., we are unconstrained in making moral decisions.[2]

In a previous book, *The Broken Gift*,[3] I explored this apparent paradox of human free will and Divine Providence. Let's review the key concepts here.[4]

Adam, Free Will, Divine Providence, and the Mission of Humanity

Adam could have obeyed the commandment to not eat the fruit, but he exercised his free will and disobeyed. As we have seen, the Divine plan must still unfold, despite his act.

How?

Adam was given one great, all-inclusive soul, wherein it was difficult to discern the parts (the individual souls) because they were bound in singular unity. That was the Divine Plan: a single, unified, rectified soul that could nullify itself and obey a 'simple' command, one such as, "Do not eat fruit from a particular tree for a mere three hours." When Adam sinned, his unified soul shattered into billions of soul sparks, each of these sparks damaged by his sin. Each spark was destined to be born in a different body, with its recognizable uniqueness and particular characteristics. Each person thus born with a soul spark, and possessing free will, can exercise this free will to rectify his own small spark of the great soul of Adam, of which it is a part. Through this rectification process, eventually all soul sparks will be repaired so they can all reunite again as one.[5]

The mission of human beings is to fulfill the Divine Plan by repairing all souls and returning them to the level of unity from which they all originated, but on a higher level.

Still, we may wrestle with the apparent paradox of human free will versus Divine Providence. The Torah's teachings regarding free will and Divine Providence can be summarized as follows:

> Free will is granted to every human being. If a person desires to take the morally right path, he has the power to do so, and he rectifies his soul spark. However, a person is also at liberty to choose the morally wrong path and cause damage.

> As individual subjects, people therefore act with unrestrained free will.[6] Our actions are voluntarily performed.

Hence, we are entirely responsible for all our behaviors. As objects of God's will, however, people are governed by Divine Providence. How—if at all—we are affected by the voluntary actions of others is determined by Divine Providence. Hence, human responsibility notwithstanding, God is the true and only cause of everything that happens to us.[7]

A fundamental belief in the law and commandments dictates that a person be judged according to his deeds. If he chooses the right moral action, he will be rewarded; if he does evil, he will be punished.[8] On the other hand, Divine Providence is always at work; the plan is Divinely ordained.

Theologically, free will is absolute; we have free choice in moral matters. Yet Divine Providence also is absolute; thus, affairs will unfold according to God's plan. And as we have seen, the Divine Plan proceeds, individually, with our free will; we affect some of its timing and details, but only in a small way.

Final Thoughts on Our Rebirth and Entry into the Seventh Millennium

In this book, I have tried to decipher the plan of human history. We have seen a clear pattern, repeated several times, to bring the plan to its conclusion, so far unsuccessfully. This time around, we are guaranteed to achieve the Divine Purpose. Why wait? Why experience more hard times? Why not hasten the process through our exercise of free will? Although individually we have some influence on the pace of the plan, collectively we definitely have the power to expedite the plan.

There is a general concept that, like human birth, all birth—including the transition to the seventh millennium—is preceded by a pregnancy and then labor. The pattern of history clearly indicates that we are nearing the end of the 'pregnancy'. Next is 'labor', the hard times (or "period of great calamities") just before the beginning of the End of Days.

It's not in vogue today, but when I was born, the smoothest route to birth was via Caesarean section—voilà, no labor, just anesthesia, a short procedure, and the child arrived. Analogously, we are guaranteed that the Divine Purpose will be achieved, and we are given certainty that we can hasten it, that we can take the smoothest route.

Returning to our earlier metaphor of the glass maze of history, we are now at the final intersection of God's plan and human action. We can see the exit through the glass panes. We can continue to navigate the maze, or we can see that this particular pane, right in front of us, has a handle to open it.

Are we going to open that door?

HAVE A QUESTION FOR DANIEL?

READY TO LEARN MORE?

Did reading this book raise more questions in your mind? Do you need clarification on any of the points Daniel outlined in this work? Then head over to Daniel's website at danielfriedmannbooks.ca for a chance to ask your questions directly and engage with one of the foremost authorities on the creation evolution debate. Once on the site you'll learn more about the author, find out how to get your copy of his previous works in this Inspired Studies series, and have a chance to explore his blog and media appearances.

ABOUT

DANIEL FRIEDMANN

Daniel Friedmann, P.Eng., M.A.Sc., a Readers' Favorite International Book Award Winner, studies the origin of the universe and life on earth. He is an expert on the creation evolution debate. He was the CEO of a global technology company for 20 years and is a student of religion. His work on reconciling the biblical account with scientific observation using his biblical clock formula has been reported in conferences, newspapers, and magazines, as well as television and radio programs.

He is the author of The Genesis One Code and The Broken Gift.

DOWNLOAD BOOKS 1 & 2

in

DANIEL FRIEDMANN'S

INSPIRED STUDIES SERIES

In Daniel Friedmann's first book, *The Genesis One Code*, he demonstrates an alignment between the dates of key events pertaining to the development of the universe and the appearance of life on Earth as described in Chapters 1 and 2 of Genesis, with those derived from scientific theory and observation. Daniel's second book, *The Broken Gift*, follows and extends the scope of *The Genesis One Code* to include the appearance and early history of humans. Both books are available for download from Amazon:

Get *Inspired Studies Book 1: The Genesis One Code* here:
https://www.amazon.com/gp/product/B00RFB4KTY

Get *Inspired Studies Book 2: The Broken Gift* here:
https://www.amazon.com/gp/product/B00RM92JS8

Appendix A

Overview Historical Timeline

Table A.1. Historical Summary[1]

Event	Biblical Year	Gregorian Calendar Year
end of the 6 Days of Creation	1	3760 BCE
Great Flood	1656	2105 BCE
Dispersion from Babel	1996	1765 BCE
Covenant with Abraham	2018	1743 BCE
Joseph becomes viceroy of Egypt	2229	1532 BCE
Jacob and his family go to Egypt	2238	1523 BCE
enslavement in Egypt begins	2332	1429 BCE
Moses sees the burning bush	2447	1314 BCE
Children of Israel leave Egypt	2448	1313 BCE
Revelation on Mount Sinai	2448	1313 BCE
Moses dies	2488	1273 BCE
Israel crosses the Jordan into Canaan	2488	1273 BCE
rule of Judges commences	2533	1228 BCE
Samson becomes leader	2810	951 BCE
Saul is appointed King	2882	879 BCE
David becomes King of Israel in Jerusalem	2892	869 BCE
Solomon becomes King	2924	837 BCE
First Temple is completed	2935	826 BCE
Isaiah begins his prophecies	3142	619 BCE
last of the 10 Tribes is exiled	3205	556 BCE
Jeremiah begins his prophecies	3298	463 BCE

Event	Biblical Year	Gregorian Calendar Year
Ezekiel prophesies in exile	3332	429 BCE
First Temple is destroyed	3338	423 BCE
Daniel prophesies	3389	372 BCE
Esther is taken to the palace	3399	362 BCE
Second Temple is completed	3412	349 BCE
Torah is translated into Greek	3515	246 BCE
Second Temple is destroyed	3829	69 CE
Talmud is complete when Ravina II dies	4235	475 CE
Arabs conquer Israel	4397	637 CE
1st Crusade destroys Jewish communities	4856	1096 CE
Rambam (Maimonides) is born	4895	1135 CE
2nd Crusade attacks Jewish communities	4907	1147 CE
Ramban is born	4954	1194 CE
Jews are expelled from England	5050	1290 CE
Black Death massacres sweep across Europe	5109	1349 CE
Jews of Spain are massacred, many outwardly convert	5151	1391 CE
Final expulsion of Jews from France	5155	1394 CE
Jews are expelled from Spain*	5252	1492 CE
Ottoman empire (Turks) conquers Israel	5276	1516 CE
Rabbi Isaac Luria is born	5294	1534 CE
Ba'al Shem Tov is born	5458	1698 CE
Jews leave Russia after wave of pogroms	5641	1881 CE
1st World War starts	5674	1914 CE

---

* As we have seen, a bad event (in this case the expulsion from Spain) leads to a new beginning. In the same year, Christopher Columbus left Spain to discover America, which is now home to half the world's Jewish population.

Event	Biblical Year	Gregorian Calendar Year
Germany starts World War II and mass killing of Jews	5699	1939 CE
Six million Jews are killed by the Nazi's during WWII	5705	1945 CE
State of Israel is established	5708	1948 CE
War of Independence ends	5709	1949 CE
Israel invades Egypt	5717	1956 CE
Jerusalem reunited under Jewish rule in Six Day War	5727	1967 CE
Yom Kippur War	5734	1973 CE
Present time	5777	2017CE

Appendix B

The Specific Pattern of History–
Elaboration

In this appendix I elaborate on the concepts presented in Chapter 4 in order to provide substantiation, with references, for the pattern of history used in this book.

To establish the pattern of history one must study in detail the sefirot and their role in time.

Patterns of 10, Seven, and Six

Since the 16th century, we have followed the sefirot scheme of Rabbi Isaac Luria (thus, the Lurianic Kabbalah). The ten sefirot are categorized as shown[1] in Table B.1.

One can see in Table B.1 that the ten sefirot are divided into three triplets of three and one final sefirah at the bottom. The triplets are positioned either right-hand, left-hand, or in the middle, at three different levels. These positions represent a mode of Divine influence within Creation.

In order to make Table B.1 more tangible and understandable, we use language and examples related to human action (versus Divine action, keeping in mind that we are created in the image of God).

Table B.1 The 10 Sefirot Categorized

Category	Sefirah			Number
	left-hand	middle	right-hand	
First triplet: In the mind	Understanding	Knowledge	Wisdom	
Second triplet: Conscious emotions (Primary emotions)	Severity	Beauty	Kindness	1 2 3
Third triplet: Conscious emotions (Secondary emotions)	Glory	Foundation	Eternity	4 5 6
Final Sefirah: Vessel to bring action		Kingship		7

The first triplet of right-hand, left-hand, and middle sefirot is the triplet associated with the mind. These three sefirot operate only within the mind—for example, when we understand a concept. The next two triplets are associated with emotions.

The second triplet of right-hand, left-hand, and middle sefirot relates to the inner emotive powers of the heart—before one begins to act and do things (e.g., emotions such as feeling kindness towards someone).

The third triplet of right-hand, left-hand, and middle sefirot is associated with action. These are also emotions, but ones that only become manifest in behavior (e.g., the feeling after an act of kindness has been performed).

The final and tenth sefirah, kingship, can be viewed as an independent entity receiving those energies that precede it. Kingship is the final result.[2]

The ten sefirot are usually numbered from 1 to 10, starting at the top right. However, since the first three sefirot associated with the mind (wisdom, understanding, and knowledge) do not manifest themselves in physical time, they are not assigned a number in Table B.1; the remaining seven sefirot (kindness, severity, beauty, eternity, glory, foundation, and kingship) are numbered 1 to 7, starting with the second triplet. This way the number of a sefirah matches the number of the corresponding Creation day and biblical millennium.

We will not elaborate on the Hebrew names of the individual ten sefirot because these are not required for our purpose of understanding the pattern of history—we only need to know the number, placement, and distribution of the numbered seven sefirot.

The sefirot in the right-hand column represent unlimited giving without taking into account the receiver, e.g., showering a child with kindness or candy. The sefirot in the left-hand column represent restraining or withdrawing, e.g., denying a child something he wants. Finally, the sefirot in the middle column represent the blend of the right-hand and left-hand sefirot—the ultimate goal, e.g., giving the child just the right amount of candy.

The last and final sefirah, kingship, is the ultimate end point. From a human perspective it is the final experience of the soul, e.g., what we experience after deciding to give, restraining the amount of giving to not overindulge the child, and then giving in a controlled way.

In Table B.1 the seven numbered sefirot correspond to physical time. In particular, sefirot 1 to 6 correspond respectively to the 6 Days of Creation, and sefirah 7 corresponds to the Sabbath.[3] Similarly, sefirot 1 to 6 correspond to the first six millennia of history, and sefirah 7 corresponds to the seventh millennium.[4]

Table B.2 shows the correspondence between sefirot 1 to 6 and (i) the 6 Days of Creation, (ii) the six millennia of history (using biblical time), and (iii) the six millennia of history (using the Gregorian calendar).

The first row of Table B.2 shows the six sefirot in succession. The second row shows the 6 Days of Creation, and the last two rows show the six millennia of history in biblical time and in Gregorian calendar years.

Table B.2   The Biblical Timeline and the Sefirot

	Second triplet			Third triplet		
Sefirah	1 Kindness right hand	2 Severity left-hand	3 Beauty middle	4 Eternity right-hand	5 Glory left-hand	6 Foundation middle
Creation Day	Day 1	Day 2	Day 3	Day 4	Day 5	Day 6
Year of history Bible time	1 to 1000	1001 to 2000	2001 to 3000	3001 to 4000	4001 to 5000	5001 to 6000
Year of history Gregorian calendar	3760 BCE to 2761 BCE	2760 BCE to 1761 BCE	1760 BCE to 761 BCE	760 BCE to 240 CE	241 CE to 1240 CE	1241 CE to 2240 CE

From Tables B.1 and B.2 we can derive the following observations:

There is a parallel between Creation Days 1 to 3 and Creation Days 4 to 6, as they correspond respectively to the second triplet and third triplet of sefirot. For example, Days 1 to 3 lead in progression to the completion of Earth, and Days 4 to 6 lead in progression to the completion of life on Earth.[5]

There is a parallel between Days 1 and 4, Days 2 and 5, and Days 3 and 6, corresponding respectively to the right-hand sefirot, left-hand sefirot, and middle sefirot. For example, in Day 1 there was light—in Day 4 there was the sun.[6] Both of these are right-hand sefirot representing giving (light). Sefirah 1 (from the second triplet) is the necessary initial creation, just light (i.e., electromagnetic radiation); sefirah 4 (from the third triplet) is light in a more usable form, i.e., the sun (see also Table 4.2).

Thus, we are starting to decipher the pattern of history. To continue deciphering, we need to use other correspondences between the sefirot and Creation. One key example relates to personalities in the Bible, and this correspondence is indicated in Table B.3.[7]

There we see that sefirot 1, 2, and 3 correspond to the Patriarchs who formed the precursors to the nation, i.e., the tribes. In particular, Jacob, the key Patriarch from whom the elemental tribes of Israel descended, occupies the key middle position of sefirah 3. Sefirot 4, 5, and 6 correspond to the personalities that formed the actual nation; again, the key middle position, sefirah 6, is occupied by Joseph, who coordinated the Israelite nation in Egypt. Finally, King David occupies sefirah 7, kingship, the ultimate goal.

Table B.3 The Sefirot and Biblical Personalities

Sefirah	Personality
1 Kindness	Abraham
2 Severity	Isaac
3 Beauty	Jacob
4 Eternity	Moses
5 Glory	Aaron
6 Foundation	Joseph
7 Kingship	David

Before we can develop the specific pattern of history, we must learn one more Kabbalistic concept: inter-inclusion, whereby each channel of Divine energy possesses within its own internal makeup something of all the other channels and is thus complete.

Inter-inclusion

We count six years and then embrace the sabbatical year.[8] But that is not the complete cycle. We then count seven cycles of sabbatical cycles, seven years seven times, or 49 years, in order to reach the completion of the cycle: the Jubilee Year.[9] As in this example, in general, completion always comes by including every sefirot manifest in each other; thus, every part reflects all the other parts.[10] A cycle of seven only becomes a complete cycle with a cycle of seven times seven, or 49.

Historical Timeline

What about human history? This is a pattern of only six sefirot (excluding the sefirot not manifested in time and the seventh sefirah). During the weekly cycle we are free to observe the Sabbath and thus create a pattern that includes the seventh sefirah, kingship. However, collectively in history, we can't do this; we cannot include kingship until after the End of Days. Thus, history proceeds over 6,000 years, and to be complete it must be an inter-inclusion of six times six, or a pattern of 36 periods.[11] An allusion to the importance of six and 36 in the Divine Plan comes from the fact that the sizes of the tablets given to Moses (the first blueprint) were six by six hand-breadths.[12]

Each 1,000 years corresponds to a sefirah, as shown in Table B.2, and each 1,000 years also inter-includes the six sefirot. Thus, each inter-included sefirah corresponds to 1,000 divided by six, or about 167[13] years. In particular, there are two parallel groupings of three sefirot (the second and third triplets), each corresponding to 500 years (i.e., three times approximately 167). Thus, each millennium has 500 years of sefirah 1, 2, and 3 and 500 years of sefirot 4, 5, and 6, with each 500 years divided into three groups of about 167 years, corresponding to each sefirah.

Table B.4 denotes the breakdown of history. Each column denotes a millennium, with the first column ranging from year 1 to 1000, and the last column ranging from year 5001 to 6000. Each row separates each millennium into six periods. Thus, for example, row one represents the first period of 167 years of each millennium, and row six, the last period of 167 years of each millennium.

Table B.4   Historical Timeline in Biblical Years

Period	Millennium					
	1st	**2nd**	**3rd**	**4th**	**5th**	**6th**
1st	1–167	1001–1167	2001–2167	3001–3167	4001–4167	5001–5167
2nd	167–333	1167–1333	2167–2333	3167–3333	4167–4333	5167–5333
3rd	333–500	1333–1500	2333–2550	3333–3500	4333–4500	5333–5500
4th	501–667	1501–1667	2501–2667	3501–3667	4501–4667	5501–5667
5th	667–833	1667–1833	2667–2833	3667–3833	4667–4833	5667–5833
6th	833–1000	1833–2000	2833–3000	3833–4000	4833–5000	5833–6000

Note: the dark gray and light gray highlighted years indicate critical periods.

To aid in referencing each cell in the historical timeline, we denote and label each cell by the number of the column, followed by a comma and the number of the row, as depicted in Table B.5. Thus, the first cell of Table B.5, cell 1,1 corresponds to years 1 to 167 (1st period—1st millennium), and the last, cell 6,6 (6th period—6th millennium), corresponds to the years 5833 to 6000.

Table B.5   Labeling of Historical Timeline

Period	Millennium					
	1st	**2nd**	**3rd**	**4th**	**5th**	**6th**
1st	1,1	2,1	3,1	4,1	5,1	6,1
2nd	1,2	2,2	3,2	4,2	5,2	6,2
3rd	1,3	2,3	3,3	4,3	5,3	6,3
4th	1,4	2,4	3,4	4,4	5,4	6,4
5th	1,5	2,5	3,5	4,5	5,5	6,5
6th	1,6	2,6	3,6	4,6	5,6	6,6

Note: the dark gray and light gray highlighted cells indicate critical periods.

Critical Periods in History

Now we have the specific pattern of six by six. When do we expect the key action in terms of achieving the goal of Creation? In Table B.1 we see that the second triplet of sefirot (sefirot 1, 2, and 3) corresponds to the primary emotions, before human action has taken place. Thus, these sefirot correspond to the creation of possibility.

In Table B.3, the first three numbered sefirot (sefirot 1, 2, and 3) in the second triplet correspond to the three Patriarchs of the nation (Abraham, Isaac, and Jacob). The third Patriarch, Jacob, is the father of the 12 Tribes of Israel. Thus, we expect the formation of the initial possibility for the purpose of the Creation to occur in cell 3,3 of Table B.5: the double occurrence of sefirah 3 (the middle sefirah of the creation of possibility). Indeed, this is the time of the Exodus and the giving of the Torah (biblical year 2448), or the law to be obeyed to bring the Divine Presence to dwell on Earth and fulfill the Divine Plan. Cells just prior to 3,3, (i.e., 3,1 and in particular 3,2) are preparation times to set the stage for cell 3,3. In cell 3,2 the nation is formed so it can receive the law in cell 3,3.

The third triplet (sefirot 4, 5, and 6) correspond to the secondary emotions, after human action has taken place. Thus, these sefirot correspond to manifestation or fulfillment. As we saw earlier, Creation Day 4 corresponded to the sun, the more usable manifestation of the light formed in Creation Day 1, so we can expect the End of Days to be in cell 6,6 of Table B.5: the double occurrence of sefirah 6 (the middle sefirah of the fulfillment of Creation), where everything that was set up in cell 3,3 with the giving of the law can culminate with the law being obeyed, leading to a house for the Lord on Earth. Cell 6,5 (just prior to cell 6,6) must be a preparatory period (i.e., 1907 CE to 2072 CE—see Table B.4).

The last cell, 6,6, is the predetermined default end of history, the End of Days. However, there are other possible cells to achieve the End of Days prior to cell 6,6. With everything arranged in cell 3,3, the first opportunity to fulfill the Divine Purpose occurs in cell 3,6—

a combination of both middle sefirot (one from the primary emotions and one from the secondary emotions); indeed, this was the time of King David and the building of the First Temple. However, the Divine Purpose was not fulfilled then.

The next opportunity to achieve the Divine Purpose occurs in cell 4,3. Why would sefirah 4 be a possibility to fulfill the Divine Purpose? Because sefirah 4 is a right-hand sefirah and represents giving, and sefirah 3 is a middle sefirah, so there is a possibility of fulfilling the Divine Purpose here. Indeed, this represents the time of the building of the Second Temple.

By the same reasoning, cell 4,6 should also represent a possibility to fulfill the Divine Purpose. Indeed, this represents a lost opportunity to build a Temple.

Any cell aligning with sefirah 5, a left-hand sefirah, which represents a contraction, does not allow any opportunity to fulfill the Divine Purpose; hence, no possibility to do so existed during the fifth millennium.

Next is the sixth millennium, with the ultimate guarantee of fulfillment of the Divine Purpose in cell 6,6.

As we move forward, we will focus our analysis only on the five critical periods represented by cells 3,3, 3,6, 4,3, 4,6, and 6,6. We line up these five critical periods and the immediate years preceding them (the preparatory time) to better discern the pattern. Thus, we have five periods of 500 years each, with each period culminating in a critical period of 167 years, highlighted in dark and light gray in Tables B.4 and B.5. This is summarized in Table B.6.

Table B.6   Critical Periods in History

Preparatory time & 1st Critical Period	Preparatory time & 2nd Critical Period	Preparatory time & 3rd Critical Period	Preparatory time & 4th Critical Period	Preparatory time & 5th Critical Period
2001 – 2167	2500 – 2667	3001 – 3167	3501 – 3667	5501 – 5667
2167 – 2333	2667 – 2833	3167 – 3333	3667 – 3833	5667 – 5833
2333 – 2500	2833 – 3000	3333 – 3500	3833 – 4000	5833 – 6000

Note: the dark gray and light gray highlighted years indicate critical periods.

The first four columns, and in particular the first four critical periods, have passed; the final column, which culminates in the fifth critical period (the End of Days), is in process.[14] The parallel structure of Table B.6, where different equivalent periods of history are shown side by side, is used to create the key tables in the book: Tables 5.1, 6.1, and 8.1.

Appendix C

Ramban on World History[1]

The following is a direct quote of Ramban's explanation of the history of the world in terms of the 6 Days of Creation.

Know that in the word *la'asoth* (to make, to do) is also included a hint that the six days of creation represent all the days of the world, i.e., that its existence will be 6 thousand years. For this reason the Rabbis have said: "A day of the Holy One, blessed be He, is a thousand years." Thus on the first 2 days the world was all water, and nothing was perfected during them. They allude to the first 2 thousand years when there was no one to call on the name of the Eternal. And so the Rabbis said: "The first 2 thousand years there was desolation." However, there was the creation of light on the first day corresponding to the thousand years of Adam who was the light of the world and who recognized his Creator. Perhaps Enosh did not worship idols until the death of the first man.

On the second day G–d said, *Let there be a firmament... and let it divide,* for on that "day" [i.e., the second thousand–year period] Noah and his sons—the righteous ones—were separated from the wicked, who were punished in water.

On the third day, the dry land appeared; plants and trees began growing, and fruits ripened. This corresponds to the third thousand–year period which begins when Abraham was 48 years old, for then he began to call the name of the Eternal. *A righteous shoot* did then spring forth in the world for he attracted many people to know the Eternal, just as the Rabbis interpreted the verse: *And the souls that they had gotten in Haran* — and he commanded his household and his children after him, *and they shall keep the way of the Eternal, to do righteousness and judgment.* This course continued until his descendants received the Torah on Sinai and the House of G–d was also built on that "day," and then all commandments—which are "the fruits" of the world—were affirmed.

Know that from the time twilight falls it is already considered as the following day. Therefore, the subject of every "day" begins somewhat before it, just as Abraham was born at the end of the second thousand years. And you will see similar examples for each and every day.

On the fourth day the luminaries—the large and the small and the stars—were created. Its "day," in the fourth thousand–year period, began 72 years after the First Sanctuary was built and continued until 172 years after the destruction of the Second Sanctuary. Now on this "day," *the children of Israel had light, for the glory of the Eternal filled the house of the Eternal,* and the light of Israel became the fire upon the altar in the Sanctuary, resting there like a lion consuming the offerings. Afterwards their light diminished and they were exiled to Babylon just as the light of the moon disappears before the birth of the new moon. Then the moon shone for them all the days of the Second Sanctuary, and the fire upon the altar rested on it like a dog. And then the two luminaries disappeared towards eventide and the Sanctuary was destroyed.

On the fifth day the waters swarmed with living creatures and fowl flying above the Earth. This was a reference to the fifth thousand–year period which began 172 years after the destruction of the Second Sanctuary since, during this millennium, the nations will have dominion, and man will be made *as the fishes of the sea, as the creeping things, that have no ruler over them; they take up all of them with the angle, catch them in their net and gather in their drag,* and no one seeks the Eternal.

On the sixth day in the morning, G–d said: *'Let the earth bring forth the living creature after its kind, cattle and creeping thing, and beast of the earth after its kind.'* Their creation took place before sunrise, even as it is written, *the sun ariseth, they withdraw, and crouch in their dens.* Then man was created in the image of G–d, and this is the time of his dominion, as it is written, *Man goeth forth unto his work and to his labor until the evening.* All this is an indication of the sixth thousand–year period in the beginning of which the "beasts," symbolizing the kingdoms *that knew not the Eternal,* will rule, but after a tenth thereof—in the proportion of the time from the first sparklings of the sun to the beginning of the day—the redeemer will come, as it is said concerning him, *And his throne is as the sun before Me.* This is the son of David, who was formed in the image of G–d, as it is written, *And behold, there came with the clouds of heaven, one like unto a son of man, and he came even to the Ancient One of days, and he was brought near before Him. And there was given him dominion, and Glory, and a kingdom.* This will take place 118 years after the completion of 5000 years, that the word of the Eternal by the mouth of Daniel might be accomplished: *And from the time that the continual burnt–offering shall be taken away, and the detestable thing that causeth appalment set up, there shall be a 1290 years.*

It would appear from the change of days—from the swarms of the waters and the fowl created on the fifth day to the beasts of the Earth created on the sixth day—that in the beginning of the sixth thousand–year period a new ruling kingdom will arise, *dreadful and terrible, and strong exceedingly,* and approaching the truth more than the preceding ones.

The seventh day which is the Sabbath alludes to the World to Come, "which will be wholly a Sabbath and will bring rest for life everlasting."

And may G–d guard us during all the days and set our portion with His servants, the blameless ones.

Glossary

Abraham: Originally called Abram, he is given the name Abraham at the Covenant described in Genesis 17. God calls Abraham to leave his land, family, and household in Mesopotamia in return for a new land, family, and inheritance in Canaan, the Promised Land. Abraham's story ends with the death and burial of his wife Sarah in the grave that he has purchased in Hebron (a town in southern Judah), followed by the marriage of his heir Isaac to a wife from his own people. These two episodes signify first, the right of his descendants to the land, and second, the exclusion of the land's previous inhabitants, the Canaanites, from Israel's patrimony. For Jews, Abraham is the first Jew, the founder of Judaism, the physical and spiritual ancestor of the Jewish people, and the first of the three Patriarchs.

Abrahamic religions: Faiths of Middle Eastern origin, emphasizing and tracing their common origin to Abraham or recognizing a spiritual tradition identified with him. They include Judaism, Christianity, and Islam.

Adam: The first created man. He looked nothing like us. Only after his sin was he diminished, thereby becoming more like us. Normal humans are referred to as humankind. Adam is referred to as Adam or man.

Agag: The name of the king of the Amalekites. Agag was taken alive by King Saul after destroying the Amalekites (I Samuel 15). His life was spared by Saul. The prophet Samuel regarded this clemency as a defiance of the will of God, which was "to completely destroy" the Amalekites. Samuel put Agag to death, but only after Agag managed to make a woman pregnant.

Amalek: A nation whose purpose is to maintain the separation between the Divine and this world. Every time we are close to achieving the Cosmic Purpose, the nation of Amalek attacks. The original Amalek was the grandson of Esau, one of the two sons of Isaac—son of Abraham.

Angel (*malach* in Hebrew): A spiritual being without physical characteristics. A messenger sent by God to perform certain tasks, such as: Michael, who is dispatched on missions that are expressions of God's kindness; Gavriel, who executes God's severe judgments; and Rafael, whose responsibility is to heal. Some angels are created for one specific task and cease to exist upon the task's completion.

Ark, Holy: Also known as the Ark of the Covenant or the Ark of the Testimony, this is a chest described in the Book of Exodus as containing the Tablets on which the 10 Commandments were inscribed.

Ba'al Shem Tov: Rabbi Yisrael ben Eliezer, born in 5458 (1698 CE) and died in 5520. During his life he founded the movement of Chasidim (his joyous expression of Judaism based on the kabbalah of the Arizal) and attracted thousands of followers (many in secret). He began teaching the concepts of Chasidut publicly in 5496.

Babel: The city, probably in present-day Iraq, where the post-Flood generation built a tower, 340 years after the Flood, and were dispersed by God after He confused their languages. Babel in Hebrew is composed of two words meaning "confusion has come."

Bar Kokhba: This name means, in Aramaic, Son of a Star. His original name was Simeon ben Kosiba. He was the leader of the last and most successful Jewish rebellion against Rome, in 132–135 CE. He died in battle when the rebellion was defeated. For a period of time Rabbi Akiba believed that perhaps he was the Messiah. Rabbi Akiba was a leading contributor to the Mishna. He is referred to in the Talmud as Head of all the Sages.

BCE: Before the Common Era.

Ben: In Hebrew, this means "son of."

Biblical years: Years as enumerated in the Bible, starting at year 1 after the creation of Adam on Day 6 and continuing to the year 6000. Biblical years correspond to Gregorian calendar (Common Era) years as follows:

Biblical Years	CE years
1	3760 BCE
1001	2760 BCE
2001	1760 BCE
3001	760 BCE
4001	241 CE
5001	1241 CE
6000	2240 CE

C-section: A surgical procedure in which incisions are made through a mother's abdomen and uterus to deliver the baby/babies.

CE: Common Era.

Commandments: 613 commandments given by God to the Jewish People (for a list, see http://www.jewfaq.org/613.htm).

Commentaries: Critical explanations or interpretations of the biblical texts.

Cosmic purpose: See Divine Purpose.

Creation: The Divine act of making something out of nothing.

Creation day: 2.54 billion years in human time.

Critical period (in history): A significant and decisive period of history in relation to achieving the Divine Purpose and reaching the End of Days.

Daniel, Book of: The book of Torah describing the experiences of Daniel and his friends in the Babylonian and Persian royal courts, as well as several of Daniel's prophecies.

David, King: King David of Israel was known for his diverse skills as both a warrior and a writer of the Psalms. In his 40 years as ruler, between 877 and 837 BCE, he united the people of Israel, led them to victory in battle, conquered lands, and paved the way for his son, Solomon, to build the Holy Temple (the First Temple). Almost all knowledge of him is derived from the books of the Prophets and Writings: Samuel I and II, Kings I, and Chronicles I. David was the eighth and youngest son of Jesse from the kingly tribe of Judah. He was also a direct descendent of Ruth the Moabite.

Diaspora, Jewish: Any place outside of the land of Israel where Jews live. The term refers to the fact that Jews were dispersed from the land of Israel—beginning within the fifth century BCE with the conquest of the ancient Kingdom of Judah by Babylon and the destruction of the First Temple, and proceeding through the time of the Jewish–Roman Wars and the destruction of the Second Temple (last war circa second century CE).

Divine Plan: God's plan for history and humanity.

Divine Providence: The notion that although human beings possess individual free will, affairs will unfold according to God's plan, i.e., the Divine Plan.

Divine Purpose: To make the physical world a dwelling-place for God.

Edom: The name given to Esau's descendants.

End of Days: Also called end time or end times, end of time, last days, final days, or eschaton, this is a time period concerned with the final events in history, described in the theologies of the dominant world religions, both Abrahamic and non-Abrahamic.

Esau: One of the two sons of Isaac, the other being Jacob. Jacob and Esau represented two critical concepts: closeness to and separation from the Creator, respectively.

Esther: A Jewish queen of the Persian king Ahasuerus. Her story is told in the Book of Esther (see Torah, The Writings), where the Jews are saved from extermination by a descendant of Amalek.

Eve: The first woman. After she sinned, Adam called her Chavah, which means the mother of mortal life.

Exile: With respect to the Jews, this refers to three conditions: (1) the people are not where they are supposed to be (their land or country), (2) the people are not together (i.e., they are scattered over many places), and (3) they are not under their own government or leadership.

Exiles, four: The Babylonian, Median, Greek, and Roman (or Edom) exiles; the last is still underway.

Exodus: The departure, under the leadership of Moses, of the Israelites from the land of Egypt. It proceeded in the following sequence:
- Moses is commanded at the burning bush, 2447.
- The Israelites leave Egypt, 2448.
- Amalek attacks.
- The Israelites cross the sea of reeds.
- Moses receives the first Tablets and the Torah, 2448, and then the second Tablets, 2449.
- The Israelites build the Tabernacle—the first dwelling place for God—2449.

Exodus, Book of: The second of the Five Books of Moses, dealing primarily with the Exodus.

Ezekiel, Book of: One of the prophetic books of the Torah. It records seven visions that the prophet Ezekiel had while exiled in Babylon.

Ezra: A scribe, spiritual and political Jewish leader, and head of the Great Assembly. A year after the completion of the Second Temple by Jews who had returned to the Land of Israel, Ezra led a second wave of exiles back from Babylon. Ezra taught and encouraged the observance of the laws of the Torah, and he copied and disseminated the books of the written Torah.

Ezra, the Book of: The book of the Torah relating Jewish history during the early Second Temple Era, under the leadership of Ezra and Nehemiah.

Free will: The notion that humans have unconstrained ability to make moral choices.

Formation: The act of taking something that already exists and making it into something else.

Genesis Flood: A large-scale flood described in Genesis that wiped out the direct descendants of Adam in the biblical year 1656–7, equivalent to 2106–5 BCE.

Gog and Magog, War of: Climactic battle against the forces of evil, whose final phase occurs in the early stages of the Messianic Era. These evil forces (Gog and Magog) presumptuously undertake to battle not only Israel but the Almighty Himself and will suffer an appropriate defeat. Gog refers to a king. Magog refers to a place, land, nation, or alliance of nations. Magog will be led by a king, Gog, who is not from Magog.

Ingathering of the Exiles: Term used to describe the redemption of Israel from exile and the return of the Jewish people to the Land of Israel.

In the image of God: This means with the power of understanding and intellect, the moral freedom and free will, and the same creative process as God.

Inter-inclusion: A concept whereby each channel of Divine energy possesses within its own internal makeup something of all the other channels and is thus complete.

Isaiah, Book of: One of the prophetic books of the Torah. It records the prophecies of Isaiah.

Isaac: The son and spiritual heir of Abraham and father of Jacob. He is the second Patriarch of Judaism.

Ishmael: The son of Abraham and Hagar. Banished together with his mother from Abraham's household because of his potentially negative influence on Isaac, he repented later in life. He is the ancestor of the Arabic nations.

Jacob: Later renamed Israel, he was the son of Isaac and the father of 12 sons who represent the tribes of Israel. He is the third Patriarch of Judaism.

Jeremiah, Book of: One of the prophetic books of the Torah. According to its opening verses, the book records the prophetic utterances of the priest Jeremiah.

Joseph: One of the sons of Jacob (Israel) and Rachel. He was sold into slavery by his jealous brothers but became powerful in Egypt and paved the way for his family's settlement there.

Jubilee Year: The year following seven cycles of Sabbatical years, which according to Torah regulations had a special impact on the ownership and management of land in the territory of the kingdoms of Israel and of Judah.

Kabbalah: Receiving or tradition; a discipline and school of thought concerned with the mystical aspect of Judaism.

Law (the law): The Five Books of Moses (see Torah).

Levi, Tribe of: Levi was one of the 12 sons of Jacob; he had three sons—Gershon, Kehas, and Merari—as well as a daughter, Yocheved. While Yocheved mothered Miriam, Moses, and Aaron (the prophetess, teacher, and High Priest of Israel, respectively), her three brothers fathered the three constituent families of the tribe of Levi. Eventually, the Levites were set apart from the rest of the Jewish people, dedicated to the Tabernacle and Temple service, assisting the Priests, the Kohanim—which was the family of Aaron.

Lubavitcher Rebbe: Menachem Mendel Schneerson (April 5, 1902– June 12, 1994), a prominent Hasidic rabbi and the seventh and last Rebbe (Hasidic leader) of the Chabad–Lubavitch. Chabad–Lubavitch is a branch of Orthodox Judaism that promotes spirituality and joy through the popularization and internalization of Jewish mysticism as the fundamental aspects of the Jewish faith movement.

Maccabees: The name of the Jewish army that revolted against the Syrian-Greek occupation in 139 BCE, whose miraculous victory culminated in the festival of Chanukah.

Maimonides: A preeminent Jewish philosopher and one of the greatest Torah scholars of the Middle Ages. See Rambam.

Maze, glass: An intricate, usually confusing network of interconnecting pathways separated by glass panes or mirrors.

Messiah (or Mashiach), Messiah ben David: A human being, the prophesied descendant of King David, who will inspire the whole world to believe in one God and usher in an era of all human beings living together in peace and brotherhood—that is, the Messianic Era.

Messiah ben Joseph: The precursor to Messiah ben David, for whose coming he will prepare the world. His principal and final function is of a political and military nature.

Messianic Era: An age where, under the leadership of the Messiah, the whole world will believe in one God and live together in peace and brotherhood; it is expected to start on or before the year 6000, or 2240 CE.

Midrash: This means exposition and denotes non-legalistic teachings of the rabbis of the Talmudic era. The plural for Midrash is Midrashim.

Midrash Rabbah: Midrash dedicated to explaining the Five Books of Moses.

Mishna: The foundation and the principal part of the Talmud, committed to writing by Rabbi Yehudah HaNasi. It was expounded in the Academies in Babylon and in Israel during the Middle Ages.

Moses: The greatest prophet of all time. Born in Egypt and raised by Pharaoh's daughter, he fled to Midian, where he married Zipporah. He was sent by God back to Egypt to liberate the Israelites. Moses visited ten plagues upon Egypt, led the Israelites out, and transmitted to them the Torah at Mount Sinai. Then he led the Israelites for 40 years while they wandered in the desert. He died in the Plains of Moab after writing the Five Books of Moses and was succeeded by his disciple Joshua, who led the Israelites into the Promised Land.

Mount Sinai: The mountain where the 10 Commandments and the Torah were given.

Nehemiah: A minister in the Persian King Artaxerxes' court, he returned to Israel in 3426 (335 BCE) to strengthen the fledgling

Jewish commonwealth. Under his leadership, the walls surrounding Jerusalem were rebuilt, increasing the city's security against its hostile neighbors. Together with Ezra, he reintroduced the observance of laws of the Torah, many of which had been forgotten in exile. The central figure of the Book of Nehemiah.

Noah: Tenth and last of the antediluvian generation heads, who was commanded to build an ark to save himself, his family, and the land animals and birds from the catastrophic Genesis Flood.

Noahide Laws: Set of moral imperatives that, according to the Talmud, were given by God as a binding set of laws for the "children of Noah"—that is, all of humanity. According to Judaism, any non-Jew who adheres to these laws is regarded as a righteous gentile and is assured of a place in the World to Come after the Messianic Era. The Seven Noahide Laws are:

1. The prohibition of idolatry.
2. The prohibition of murder.
3. The prohibition of theft.
4. The prohibition of sexual immorality.
5. The prohibition of blasphemy.
6. The prohibition of eating flesh taken from an animal while it is still alive.
7. The requirement of maintaining courts to provide legal recourse.

Oral Law: Used to interpret and apply the Written Law. It is now documented in writing. It consists primarily of the Talmud, Explanations, Midrashim, and the Zohar.

Preparatory period (in history): A significant period of history preceding a critical period.

Rabbi Isaac Luria: Known as the Arizal or Ari (1534–1572 CE) and considered the father of contemporary Kabbalah. His teachings are referred to as Lurianic Kabbalah; these describe new, coherent doctrines of the origins of Creation and its cosmic rectification, while incorporating a recasting and fuller systemization of preceding Kabbalistic teaching.

Rambam: Rabbi Mosheh ben Maimon, called Moses Maimonides and known by his acronym RaMBaM (1135–1204 CE), was a preeminent medieval Jewish philosopher and astronomer and one of the most prolific and influential Torah scholars and physicians of the Middle Ages in Morocco and Egypt.

Ramban: Nahmanides, also known as Rabbi Moses ben Nachman Girondi, Bonastrucça Porta, and by his acronym RaMBaN (1194–1270 CE); a leading medieval scholar, rabbi, philosopher, physician, and biblical commentator.

Rashi: Shlomo Yitzhaki (1040–1105 CE), better known by the acronym Rashi (RAbbi SHlomo Itzhaki), was a medieval French rabbi famed as the author of the first comprehensive commentary on the Talmud as well as a comprehensive commentary on the Written Law (including Genesis).

Redemption of Israel: See Ingathering of the Exiles.

Resurrection of the dead: Refers to a specific event in the future when the dead will be brought back to life.

Sabbatical Year: This is *shmita* in Hebrew, literally "release"; the seventh year of the seven-year agricultural cycle mandated by the Torah for the Land of Israel.

Samson: The seventh of the Judges of the Israelites mentioned in the Torah (Book of Judges, Chapters 13 to 16). Samson was given supernatural strength (despite being lame in both legs) by God in order to combat his enemies. He single-handedly terrorized the occupying Philistines. He was the wisest of the wise in his generation.

He became leader in 2810, and in 2831 at a pagan festival, Samson knocked down the pillars supporting the building, killing himself and thousands of Philistines. After his death the Philistines remained subdued for 20 years until they were sure he had no descendants who had inherited his strength.

Sanhedrin: The "Supreme Court" of the ancient Jewish state, in the tradition established in Exodus, Chapter 18. According to tradition, the Oral Torah was given to Moses and passed on a continuous line to Joshua, then to the elders, then to the prophets, and then to the Sanhedrin. The Sanhedrin decided difficult cases and cases of capital punishment. It also fixed the calendar, taking testimony to determine when a new month began.

Saul, King: Righteous member of the Tribe of Benjamin. He was anointed by Samuel (the last of the Judges) as the first Israelite king in 2882 (879 BCE). When he failed to destroy Amalek as commanded by God, Samuel anointed David in his stead. Overcome with jealousy, Saul pursued David until he himself was killed in battle by the Philistines.

Sefirah (plural Sefirot): A channel of Divine energy or life force. There are 10 sefirot. It is via the 10 sefirot that God interacts with Creation; they may thus be considered His attributes.

Sefirot: See Sefirah.

Seventh Millennium: The beginning of the era of universal reward, known as the World to Come, that follows the End of Days, or the Messianic Era. The seventh millennium is also referred to as The Millennium by some Christian denominations.

Sin: Adam's sin or primordial sin, wherein Adam ate the forbidden fruit of the Tree of Knowledge of Good and Evil. This sin occurred three hours before the end of Day 6.

Solomon, King: Son of King David and Bathsheba, appointed king over Israel at the age of 12. He built the First Temple in Jerusalem. During his reign, the Israelites enjoyed unprecedented peace and prosperity; they were feared and respected by the neighboring nations. The wisest man of all times, his superlative wisdom is recorded in the books of Song of Songs, Proverbs, and Ecclesiastes.

Tabernacle: Temporary, mobile sanctuary (portable version of the Temple) constructed by the Jewish People during their journey in the desert from Egypt to the land of Israel, and which continued to serve in the land of Israel until it was destroyed a few hundred years before the First Temple was constructed in Jerusalem.

Tablets: Two stone Tablets of Testimony on which the 10 Commandments were engraved. There were two sets of Tablets. The first Tablets were made by God and inscribed *"by the finger of God"* (Exodus 31:18). When Moses descended the mountain with the first Tablets and saw that the people had committed the sin of worshipping the Golden Calf, *"he threw down the tablets from his hands and shattered them at the foot of the mountain"* (Exodus 32:19). The second Tablets, given after the sin of the Golden Calf, were of a lower level; the script was God's but the stones were carved by Moses. The first Tablets were not totally lost, as Moses was instructed to place their broken fragments into the Holy Ark along with the second Tablets.

Talmud: Meaning instruction, learning; a central text of mainstream Judaism in the form of a record of rabbinic discussions pertaining to Jewish law, ethics, philosophy, customs, and history.

Temple, First and Second: These were the central sanctuaries in Jerusalem that served as the physical abode of the indwelling of God's Presence on Earth and as the venue for the sacrificial service. The First Temple was built by King Solomon (826 BCE) and destroyed by the Babylonians (423 BCE); the Second Temple was built by Nehemiah (349 BCE), remodeled by Herod, and destroyed by the Romans (69 CE); the third, eternal Temple will be built by the Messiah.

Theocracy: Form of government in which a state is understood as governed under Torah law by officials who are regarded as Divinely guided. In Greek the term means "rule of God," and it was used by Josephus Flavius for the kingdoms of Israel and Judah.

This World: The 6,000 years of history post Eden, culminating in the End of Days. It is followed by the World to Come and preceded by the 6 Days of Creation and existence in the Garden of Eden.

Tikkun: Hebrew for rectification.

Torah: Consists of both the Written Law and the Oral Law (see separate entries). The Written Law itself consists of the following:

The Five Books of Moses (The Law):
- Bereishith (In the beginning) (Genesis)
- Shemoth (The names) (Exodus)
- Vayiqra (And He called) (Leviticus)
- Bamidbar (In the wilderness) (Numbers)
- Devarim (The words) (Deuteronomy)

NEVI'IM (The Prophets):
- Yehoshua (Joshua)
- Shoftim (Judges)
- Shmuel (I &II Samuel)
- Melakhim (I & II Kings)
- Yeshayah (Isaiah)
- Yirmyah (Jeremiah)
- Yechezqel (Ezekiel)
- The Twelve (treated as one book)
  - Hoshea (Hosea)
  - Yoel (Joel)
  - Amos
  - Ovadyah (Obadiah)
  - Yonah (Jonah)

- o Mikhah (Micah)
- o Nachum
- o Chavaqquq (Habbakkuk)
- o Tzefanyah (Zephaniah)
- o Chaggai
- o Zekharyah (Zechariah)
- o Malakhi

KETHUVIM (The Writings):
- Divrei Ha–Yamim (The words of the days) (Chronicles)
- Tehillim (Psalms)
- Iyov (Job)
- Mishlei (Proverbs)
- Ruth
- Shir Ha–Shirim (Song of Songs)
- Qoheleth (the author's name) (Ecclesiastes)
- Eikhah (Lamentations)
- Esther
- Daniel
- Ezra and Nechemyah (Nehemiah) (treated as one book)

Tribes, 10: The tribes that lived in northern Israel (all except (Judah and Benjamin) and were dispersed as a result of Assyrian (approx. 556 BCE) conquest and thus "lost."

Tribes, 12: The tribes formed in the main by the natural increase of the offspring of Jacob. The descendants of each of his sons are believed to have held together and thus constituted a social entity.

Universal timeline: The pattern of the Divine Plan of history—that is, the default pattern.

World to Come: The time that comes after the End of Days, the seventh millennium being its first stage. It is preceded by this world.

Zohar: Meaning splendor, radiance; it is the foundational work in the literature of Jewish mystical thought known as Kabbalah.

Endnotes

A NOTE FROM THE AUTHOR

1   Julius Müller, *Chucpedie* (Czech Republic, Garamond 2011), p. 124.

CHAPTER 1

1   These are described in texts generally known as apocalypses (a Greek word meaning revelations). Apocalypses are characterized by a triumphant movement from cataclysm to utopia, from suffering on Earth to the restoration of peace and harmony. Suffering in these books can reach unimaginable heights, but the entire course of events is directed by God, who is sovereign over his creation and will reward those who remain faithful to him. This suffering is overseen by God, who will soon bring it to an end before setting up his utopian kingdom.

2   Rabbi Nosson Scherman/Meir Zlotowitz, General Editors, *Daniel / A New Translation with a Commentary anthologized from Talmudic, Midrashic and Rabbinic Sources* (New York: Mesorah Publications Ltd., Second Edition Seventh Impression 2006); An Overview/Daniel—A Bridge to Eternity by Rabbi Nosson Scherman.

3   Isaiah 2:4.

4   Aryeh Kaplan, *The Real Messiah?: A Jewish Response to Missionaries,* (New York, National Conference of Synagogue Youth/Union of Orthodox Jewish Congregations of America, 1985).

5   Deuteronomy 31:29; also see Ezekiel 38 and 39.

[6] On the one hand, everything is preordained and proceeding according to a plan; on the other, we have complete free will. Thus, the plan of history proceeds, and we can influence its timing and exact course: individually in a small way, or collectively in a bigger way.

[7] There are hundreds of references for this notion. See a short summary at www.aish.com/ci/a/48925077.html

[8] "The general rule regarding prophesy is that negative prophesies do not have to take place if the people mend their ways, while good prophesies are guaranteed to become manifest." Yitzchak Ginsburgh, *Mashiach and Jewish Leadership: Part 37—The Second and Third Stages of Mashiach*, Gal Einai Publication Society, 1996–2011, http://www.inner.org/LEADER/leader37.htm

[9] *"God looked into the Torah and created the world."* Midrash Rabbah on Genesis 1:2; Zohar I:134a, Vol. II, 161b.

[10] Rashi (the most famous Torah commentator) on Genesis 31:18 explains that God gave Moses the whole Torah—not just the two Tablets containing the 10 Commandments. In addition, the 10 Commandments encompass all 613 commandments (Rashi on Exodus 24:12).

[11] Many Muslims believe the Judeo–Christian scriptures have been corrupted and are therefore inaccurate views of the actual revelations of Moses, David, and Christ.

[12] The Torah comprises the Written Law—the Five Books of Moses, Prophets, Writings (i.e., Psalms), Sanhedrin, Rabbinical Laws and Customs—and the Oral Law: Talmud (Mishna, Gemarah), Explanations, Midrashim, Zohar. All biblical quotes and commentaries (unless otherwise referenced) are from translations found in *The Stone Edition Chumash, the Torah, Haftaros, and Five*

Megillos, with a Commentary from Rabbinic Writings, General Editors Rabbi Nosson Scherman and Rabbi Meir Zlotowitz (New York: Mesorah Publications Ltd., 2009). All Talmud quotes are from the English translations found in *Soncino Babylonian Talmud*, Ed. Rabbi Dr. I. Epstein (London: The Soncino Press, 1935–1948).

13   Midrash Rabbah on Genesis 1:2; Zohar I:134a, Vol. II, 161b.

14   See Chapter 3, Isaiah 60:22.

15   See Chapter 3, Isaiah 48:11. Ezekiel 20:9.

16   Babylonian Talmud, Rosh Hashana 31a and Sanhedrin 97a.

17   George Musser, "Could Time End?" *Scientific American,* 303 (3), September 2010, pp. 84–91.

18   Ibid.

19   Avraham Sutton, *Spiritual Technology,* (New York: Shamir Inc., 2013), Appendix II.

20   Eliezer Zeiger, "Time, Space and Consciousness," BOr HaTorah Vol. 15, ed. Prof. Herman Branover (Israel: SHAMIR, 2005).

21   Zohar Vayera 119a. Ramban on Genesis 2:3 maintains that the seven days of creation correspond to the seven millennia of the existence of natural creation. The tradition teaches that the seventh day of the week, Shabbat, or the day of rest, corresponds to the Great Shabbat, the seventh millennium (years 6000–7000), the age of universal rest.

22   (i) Daniel Friedmann, *The Genesis One Code* (USA: Inspired Books, 2014).

(ii) Daniel Friedmann, *The Broken Gift* (USA: Inspired Books, 2013).

23   Daniel Friedmann, *The Genesis One Code* (USA: Inspired Books, 2014), Appendix B.

24   Most estimates of the biblical period prior to the Common Era, according to biblical eschatology experts, are around 4000 BCE. Bishop Ussher' (17th-century Church of Ireland) proposed a date of 4004 BCE, which has been treated as authoritative by many, but it differs from other biblically based estimates, such as those of Jose ben Halafta (3761 BCE) and Bede (3952 BCE). This book uses a chronology developed from Torah sources; see endnote 27 of this chapter.

25   Rabbi Aryeh Kaplan, *Sefer Yetzirah, The Book of Creation: revised edition* (San Francisco; Weiser Books, 1997), p. 189.

26   Note that although scripture contains a history and timeline, it does not always follow chronological order.

27   (i) Mattis Kantor, *The Jewish Time Line Encyclopedia* (New Jersey, Jason Aronson Inc., 1992).

      (ii) There is a discrepancy (of about 165 years) between the biblically derived timeline and the secular timeline based on the dating of the destruction of the First Temple; the Talmudic chronology places the destruction of the First Temple in 3338 or 423 BCE and the modern secular dating for it in 587 BCE. This issue is not resolved. This book relies exclusively on the biblical timeline as detailed in Mattis Kantor's exhaustive and well-referenced book—both for the 6,000-year biblical calendar and the corresponding Gregorian calendar.

28   (i) Exile in this context refers to three conditions: (i) the people are not where they are supposed to be (i.e., they are not in their land or their country); (ii) the people are not together (i.e., they are scattered over many places); and (iii) they are not under their own government or leadership.

(ii) Although the various exiles seem to happen as a result of external events, such as conquests, the sources teach that *"exile comes to the world for idolatry, for incest, for murder, and for not leaving the earth at rest during the Sabbatical year"* (Ethics of our Fathers 5:9). The current exile is attributed to the sin of *"hatred without cause,"* which is said to be as grave as idolatry, incest, and murder (Babylonian Talmud Yoma 9b).

[29] The 12 Tribes are usually divided along the 12 sons of Jacob. However, when it comes to the division of the territory or land, Joseph's two sons (Ephraim and Manasseh) are counted as separate tribes, making the total number of tribes thirteen. There were, however, only 12 territorial allotments, as the tribe of Levi had no designated territory and lived amongst the other tribes.

[30] The tribes are "lost" in the sense that their whereabouts are unknown to the world at large, even if they themselves have maintained their identity. *The Essential Malbim* (New York: Mesorah Publications Ltd., 2009), pp. 331-332.

[31] *"Then he led away into exile all Jerusalem and all the captains and all the mighty men of valor, ten thousand captives, and all the craftsmen and the smiths. None remained except the poorest people of the land"* 2 Kings 24:14-16.

[32] These tribes (Yehuda and Benjamin) are not lost, since their whereabouts are known; yet they are dispersed throughout the world. *The Essential Malbim* (New York: Mesorah Publications Ltd., 2009), pp. 331- 332.

[33] Cynthia R. Chapman, *The World of Biblical Israel, Course Guidebook* (USA: The Teaching Company, 2013), Lecture 1.

34   Examples:

(a) the Egyptian victory stele (an upright stone slab or column typically bearing a commemorative inscription or relief design) of Pharaoh Merneptah, dating to around 1200 BCE.

(b) the Black Obelisk of Assyrian King Shalmaneser III.

(c) the Cyrus cylinder, a clay cylinder inscribed with cuneiform text in the Akkadian language of the Babylonians. For example, this cylinder provides independent Persian evidence for the policy of repatriating conquered peoples and sponsoring the rebuilding of local shrines and temples. Biblical sources describe the return of some of the Babylonian exiles under a Persian-sponsored policy of repatriation and rebuilding. The Book of Ezra announces this return by quoting an imperial decree. In the Bible, the quoted edict comes about not because Cyrus had independent ideas or policymaking skills, but because God had announced through his prophet Jeremiah that He would bring the exiles back.

35   Ramban on Genesis 2:3.

CHAPTER 2

1   Likkutei Amarim, Tanya, ch. 36, paraphrasing Midrash Tanchuma, Parshas Naso, sec. 16. The word for "desired" used by the statement comes from the root (in Hebrew) taavah, which connotes a supra-rational desire. There is no logical explanation as to why God desired "a dwelling in the lowly realms"; we only know that He desired it, and that the satisfaction of this desire is the ultimate purpose of creation.

2   Rabbi Nissan Dovid Dubov, *To Live And Live Again, An Overview of Techiyas Hameisim, Based On The Classical Sources And On The Teachings Of Chabad Chassidism* (USA, Sichos In English, 1988–

2009), Chapter 2, The Purpose of Creation, http://www.sichos-in-english.org/books/to-live-and-live-again/03.htm

[3] Babylonian Talmud Sanhedrin 105a. The Talmud states: *"Righteous people of all nations have a share in the world to come* [the world after this one, i.e., the seventh millennium]." Any non-Jew who lives according to these laws is regarded as one of *"the righteous among the gentiles."*

[4] "Universal Morality: The Seven Noahide Laws," Chabbad.org, http://www.chabad.org/therebbe/article_cdo/aid/62221/jewish/Universal-Morality.htm

[5] (i) The source for the laws: Genesis 9:4–6, Babylonian Talmud Sanhedrin 56a. The laws are derived exegetically from Divine demands addressed to Adam and Noah, the progenitors of all mankind, and are thus regarded as universal.

(ii) The explanation of the laws: "Universal Morality: The Seven Noahide Laws," Chabbad.org, http://www.chabad.org/therebbe/article_cdo/aid/62221/jewish/Universal-Morality.htm

[6] Babylonian Talmud Sanhedrin 37a.

[7] Isaiah 42:6.

[8] "Universal Morality: The Seven Noahide Laws," Chabbad.org, http://www.chabad.org/therebbe/article_cdo/aid/62221/jewish/Universal-Morality.htm

[9] The 613 commandments are delineated in the Torah and compiled by the Rambam in *Mishneh Torah*. For a list see http://www.jewfaq.org/613.htm.

[10] The 10 Commandments encompass all 613 commandments. Rashi on Exodus 24:12.

[11] 369 of the commandments can be observed today outside of Israel. Eliezer Danzinger, "How Many of the Torah"s Commandments Still Apply?", Chabbad.org http://www.chabad.org/library/article_cdo/aid/541686/jewish /How-Many-of-the-Torahs-Commandments-Still-Apply.htm

[12] In Hebrew, "Kashrus," from the root kosher (or "kasher"), means suitable and/or pure, thus ensuring fitness for consumption. The laws of "Kashrus" include a comprehensive legislation concerning permitted and forbidden foods and how those foods must be prepared and eaten.

[13] In the Messianic Era, once the theocratic state of Israel is established and the Temple is rebuilt, all 613 commandments will be observable.

[14] "The Rebbe and President Ronald Reagan," Chabbad.org, http://www.chabad.org/therebbe/article_cdo/aid/142535/jewi sh/The-Rebbe-and-President-Reagan.htm

[15] Exodus 15:18.

[16] Zechariah 14:9.

[17] Exodus Midrash Rabbah 32:1.

[18] Enosh was the son of Seth, who was Adam's child, born 130 years after Cain and Able. It was in the days of Enosh that idolatry began to surface and spread in the world.

[19] (i) Genesis Midrash Rabbah 19:17.
(ii) Nissan Dovid Dubov, "Adam", Chabad–Lubavitch Media Center, 1993–2014. http://www.chabad.org/library/article_cdo /aid/361873/jewish/Adam.htm

(iii) It must be noted that the concept of "removal of the Divine Presence" does not suggest that God actually removed Himself from the world. Rather, the removal of the Divine Presence refers to the insensitivity of the world population to Godliness. The pattern is clear: sin creates insensitivity. However, the righteous re-sensitize the world to its true reality. In Kabbalah, this is referred to as *Tikkun Olam*, or the "rectification of the world." The purpose is to return the world to its perfect state as it was before the primordial sin.

[20] Ibid. (i), (ii).

[21] Lubavitcher Rebbe, "Chassidic Insights for Parshah Lech–Lecha," Chabad–Lubavitch Media Center, 1993–2014, Chapter 12, http://www.chabad.org/parshah/article_cdo/aid/758932/jewish/Chassidic-Insights.htm:

> *God gave us the first Temple based on the premise that we would observe His commandments faithfully and completely. When we sinned, the first Temple was destroyed and subsequently replaced by the second Temple, which was based on the premise of repentance. The third Temple will be built in the messianic era, when our physical senses will be so refined that they will perceive Divinity as readily as they presently perceive physical matter (see Isaiah 52:8).*

[22] (i) Ibid.

(ii) Zechariah 13:2.

[23] Daniel Friedmann, *The Broken Gift* (USA: Inspired Books, 2013), pp. 95–96 (on the animalistic soul).

[24] The eternal struggle with Amalek is described in Exodus and Deuteronomy:

> *God said to Moses, "Write this as remembrance in the Book and recite it in the ears of Joshua, that I shall surely erase the memory of Amalek from under the heavens." Moses built an altar and called its name "God is my miracle;" and he said, "For the hand is on the throne of*

God: God maintains a war against Amalek, from generation to generation." (Exodus 17:14–16).

Remember what Amalek did to you, on the way, when you were leaving Egypt, that he happened upon you on the way, and he struck those of you who were hindmost, all the weaklings at your rear, when you were faint and exhausted, and he did not fear God. It shall be that when God, your God, gives you as an inheritance to possess it, you shall wipe out the memory of Amalek from under the heaven—you shall not forget! (Deuteronomy 25:17–19).

25   For Amalek's genealogy, see Genesis 36:11.

26   For the struggle between Jacob and Esau, see Genesis 25:19–33:20 and the elaboration in Rabbi Meir Zlotowitz, Bereishis, *Genesis: A New Translation with a Commentary Anthologized from Talmudic Midrashic and Rabbinic Sources* (NY: Mesorah Publications Ltd., 1977), p. 1021.

27   Exodus 17:8–15.

28   Obadiah 1:18

29   "Battles with Amalek," adapted by Moshe Yakov Wisnefsky from *Sichot Kodesh* 5739, vol. 2, pp. 144–45, 7; *Sefer HaMa'amarim* 5742, pp. 101–2 & 5744, pp. 165–166; *Likutei Sichot*, vol. 1, p. 144 & vol. 26, pp. 87–88; *Hitva'aduyot* 5745, vol. 2, pp. 1363–1364.
http://www.chabad.org/kabbalah/article_cdo/aid/380224/jewish/Battles-with-Amalek.htm

30   Exodus 17:14.

31   Exodus 17:16.

32   I Samuel 15:4.

[33] I Samuel 15:14–27. Even though the prophet Samuel finished the job by killing Agag (see I Samuel 15:33), in the intervening period Agag had a relationship from which a son was born.

[34] Esther Midrash Rabbah 7:23.

[35] (i) Exodus 17:14.

(ii) *The Stone Edition Chumash, the Torah, Haftaros, and Five Megillos, with a Commentary from Rabbinic Writings*, General Editors Rabbi Nosson Scherman and Rabbi Meir Zlotowitz (New York: Mesorah Publications Ltd., 2009), p. 145.

> *The Four Kingdoms/Exiles: Jacob [in his dream—Genesis 28:12] was shown the guardian angels of the Four Kingdoms that would ascend to dominate Israel. Jacob saw each angel climbing a number of rungs corresponding to the years of its dominion, and then descending, as its reign ended: Babylon's [the first kingdom] angel climbed seventy rungs and then went down; Media's angel [climbed] fifty-two [rungs]; Greece's [angel climbed] 130 [rungs]—but the angel of Edom/Esau kept climbing indefinitely, symbolizing the current exile [initiated by Rome], which seems to be endless. Jacob was frightened, until God assured him that he would receive Divine protection and eventually return to the Land.*

(iii) The Egyptian exile was not included in the vision of the Four Kingdoms; it was prophesied to Jacob separately (Genesis 15:13) because it was an exile of a different type: Egypt was the necessary prerequisite to nationhood, not an aggressive interruption of Israel's independent status. Rabbi Meir Zlotowitz, Bereishis, *Genesis: A New Translation with a Commentary Anthologized from Talmudic Midrashic and Rabbinic Sources* (NY: Mesorah Publications Ltd., 1977), p. 418.

CHAPTER 3

1   Isaiah 48:11.

2   Ezekiel 20:9.

3   Pesachim 54b; Midrash Tehilim 9:2. See also http://www.chabad.org/library/moshiach/article_cdo/aid/101 680/jewish/Date-of-Mashiachs-Coming.htm

4   Isaiah 60:22.

5   Rabbi Jacob Immanuel Schochet, *Mashiach: The Principle of Mashiach and the Messianic Era in Jewish Law and Tradition, Expanded Edition,* (USA: Sichos in English, 1988–2009). Date of Mashiach"s Coming. http://www.sichosinenglish .org/books/mashiach/05.htm#n71.

6   Babylonian Talmud Sanhedrin 98a.

> *R. Alexandri said: R. Joshua b. Levi pointed out a contradiction. It is written, in its time [will the Messiah come], whilst it is also written, I [the Lord] will hasten it! (Isaiah 60:22)—if they are worthy, I will hasten it: if not, [he will come] at the due time. R. Alexandri said: R. Joshua opposed two verses: it is written, And behold, one like the son of man came with the clouds of heaven (Daniel 7:13)[i.e. miraculously] whilst [elsewhere] it is written, [behold, thy king cometh unto thee ...] lowly, and riding upon an ass! (Zechariah 9:7) [i.e. naturally]—if they are meritorious, [he will come] with the clouds of heaven; if not, lowly and riding upon an ass.*

7   Babylonian Talmud Sanhedrin 98a.

8   Aryeh Kaplan, *The Real Messiah?: A Jewish Response to Missionaries* (New York, National Conference of Synagogue Youth/Union of Orthodox Jewish Congregations of America, 1985), Chapter 9.

9   Babylonian Talmud Sotah 49b.

10   (i) Rabbi Jacob Immanuel Schochet, *Mashiach: The Principle of Mashiach and the Messianic Era in Jewish Law and Tradition, Expanded Edition,* (USA: Sichos in English, 1988–2009). Ikvot Meshicha: The Time Immediately Before Mashiach, http://www.sichos-in-english.org/books/mashiach/03.htm

(ii) Babylonian Talmud Sotah 49b.

(iii) *""And I shall leave amongst you of the nation, poverty and destitution, and you will yearn for, and trust in God".*" Zephaniah 3:12.

11   (i) Ibid. (i).

(ii) Babylonian Talmud Sanhedrin 97a; and Shir Rabba 2:29 (Haggadic Midrash on Song of Songs).

12   Ibid. (i).

13   Ibid. (i).

14   (i) Ibid. (i).

(ii) Zohar I:118a.

15   Aryeh Kaplan, *The Real Messiah?: A Jewish Response to Missionaries* (New York, National Conference of Synagogue Youth/Union of Orthodox Jewish Congregations of America, 1985), pp. 89–90.

16   Ezekiel 36.8.

17   Ezekiel 36:22–25.

18   Numbers 24:17. Note Seth was Adam's third son, from whom all humanity descends.

19   (i) Ezekiel 38–39, Isaiah 66.

20   Ezekiel 38, 39.

21   Esther Midrash Rabbah 7:23.

22   Meaning two conditions: (1) all the people will be brought back to the land of Israel from their various places of exile and (2) they will have their own theocratic government. All the people means the 10 lost tribes as well as the other two dispersed tribes.

23   Deuteronomy 30:3–5.

24   (i) Ezekiel 20:32–37, 40–42.

      (ii) Similar text can be found in Isaiah 27:13.

      It shall come to pass on that day that a great shofar shall be sounded [Messianic era], and those lost in the land of Assyria and those exiled in the land of Egypt shall come, and they shall prostrate themselves before the Lord on the holy mount in Jerusalem.

25   Ezekiel 37:26–28.

26   Isaiah 56:7.

27   Zechariah 14:9.

28   Isaiah 11:9.

29   There are different opinions as to how the physical process of resurrection will take place: either a new body will grow organically or bones will rise and recover their flesh. The physical resurrection may happen anywhere in the world; the actual restoration of the soul to the body will only take place in

(ii) Gog refers to a king. Magog refers to a place, land, or nation or an alliance of nations. The alliance of nations, Magog (descendants of Amalek), will be led by a king, Gog, who is not necessarily from Magog.

the Land of Israel. Written by Rabbi David Sedley and Edited by the Morasha Curriculum Team, "The World to Come: Part I, " NLE Resources, Jerusalem. http://nleresources.com/nle-morasha-syllabus/spirituality-and-kabbalah/the-world-to-come-iii-the-new-you-resurrection-of-the-dead/.

[30] From a translation of the full text of the 13 foundations of Jewish belief, compiled by Rabbi Moshe ben Maimon; foundation/principle thirteen.

[31] Exodus 6:3–4.

[32] Babylonian Talmud Sanhedrin 90b.

[33] Isaiah 26:19.

[34] Ezekiel 37:12–14.

[35] Genesis Midrash Rabbah 95.

[36] Ramban, *Commentary on the Torah*, translated by Rabbi Dr. Charles B. Chavel (NY: Shilo Publishing House, 1971), Deuteronomy 30:6.

[37] Rabbi Moshe ben Maimon (Rambam), *Mishneh Torah*, Laws of Kings 12:5.

[38] (i) Isaiah 35:5–6.

(ii) Note that the cures described in Isaiah are believed to result from advances in technology rather than miracles involving changes in the laws of nature. Aryeh Kaplan, *The Real Messiah?: A Jewish Response to Missionaries* (New York, National Conference of Synagogue Youth/Union of Orthodox Jewish Congregations of America, 1985), Chapter 9.

[39] Isaiah 25:8.

40 Isaiah 61:5.

41 For example, one opinion is that Messiah ben Joseph will be well versed in Torah: *"to the degree that we are drawn ever closer to the Complete Redemption during the preparatory period of the pre-Messianic Era the Torah of our righteous Messiah will be revealed little by little to select individuals by Messiah ben Joseph."* Quoted from the Gra-Gaon Rabbenu Eliyahu or Vilna Gaon. Avraham Sutton, *Spiritual Technology,* (New York: Shamir Inc., 2013), pp. 201–202.

42 Rabbi Jacob Immanuel Schochet, *Mashiach: The Principle of Mashiach and the Messianic Era in Jewish Law and Tradition, Expanded Edition,* (USA: Sichos in English, 1988–2009). Appendix II Mashiach Ben Yossef,
http://www.sichos-in-english.org/books/mashiach/11.htm

43 Rabbi Jacob Immanuel Schochet, *Mashiach: The Principle of Mashiach and the Messianic Era in Jewish Law and Tradition, Expanded Edition,* (USA: Sichos in English, 1988–2009). *Mishneh Torah,* Hilchot Melachim — Laws Concerning Kings, Chapter XI,
http://www.sichos-in-english.org/books/mashiach/09.htm

44 Deuteronomy 4:2. See also Deuteronomy 13:1.

45 *Mishneh Torah,* Hilchot Melachim—Laws Concerning Kings, Chapter X. The fact that the Messiah does not have to perform miracles is learned from Rabbi Akiva, who was a great sage of the Mishna. Rabbi Akiva and all the wise men of his generation considered King Bar Koziba to be the Messianic King without asking him for any sign or wonder of proof. Bar Koziba was killed (133 CE), and the sages then realized that he was not the Messiah. This period of history will be covered in Chapter 5.

46 *Mishneh Torah,* Hilchot Melachim—Laws Concerning Kings, Chapter X.

CHAPTER 4

[1] *"And God said, 'Let us make man in our image, after our likeness.'"* Genesis 1:26.

[2] Rabbi Meir Zlotowitz, *Bereishis, Genesis/A New Translation with a Commentary Anthologized from Talmudic Midrashic and Rabbinic Sources* (New York: Mesorah Publications, Ltd., 1977), p. 70 on Genesis 1:26.

[3] This concept is contained in Exodus 10:2, which occurs just before the eighth plague,

> *...and so that you may relate in the ears of your son and your son's son that I made a mockery of Egypt and my signs that I placed among them—that you may know that I am God.*

The commentators elaborate on this verse to explain that God guides history, "that the Exodus was a seminal event in world history because it demonstrated God's mastery over nature. Thus, it became the textbook lesson for humanity that God is not an aloof Creator, but the Master of the universe day by day and event by event. This verse encapsulates that concept, for it tells Israel that the miracles of the Exodus were to teach them for all generations that God can toy with the most powerful kingdoms, and that this creates the perception that he is YHWH, the name that denotes his eternity, because its letters comprise the word 'He was, He is, He will be.'" See Rabbi Meir Zlotowitz, *Bereishis, Genesis/A New Translation with a Commentary Anthologized from Talmudic Midrashic and Rabbinic Sources* (New York: Mesorah Publications, Ltd., 1977), p. 341 on Exodus 10:2.

[4] David Schulman, *The Sefirot: Ten Emanations of Divine Power* (London: Jason Aronson Inc., 1996), Introduction.

[5]   Leviticus 25:3–5.

[6]   Drushei Olam HaTohu 2:151b.

> *This is why so much time must transpire from the time of creation until the time of the tikkun [meaning rectification which is due to be completed when the Messiah comes]. All the forces of Gevurot [referring to God absolute power specially to revive the dead] are rooted in the six Sefirot ... which are the six days of creation ... and also the 6000 years of history that the world will exist. And within [the six Sefirot] are the roots of all that will happen from the six days of creation until the Final Tikkun...*

[7]   Nissan Mindel, *Talks and Tales* (NY: Merkos L'inyonei Chinuch, 2003).

[8]   Ramban, *Commentary on the Torah*, translated by Rabbi Dr. Charles B. Chavel (NY: Shilo Publishing House, 1971), Genesis, pp. 61–64.

[9]   Leviticus 25:3–5.

[10] Yitzchak Ginsburgh, "The Unifications of the Emotive Sefirot", Gal Einai Publication Society, 1996–2011, http://www.inner.org/kabbalah/intermediate/unification-emotive-Sefirot.php

[11] Leviticus 25:8–13.

[12] The biblical New Year can occur anytime between September 5th and October 5th; thus, the biblical year 5667 started in 1907 CE and finished in 1908 CE. For simplicity, when converting 5667 into Gregorian calendar years we use the earlier year only, i.e., 1907 CE. When an exact date is converted, it is converted accurately, e.g., early 5667 converts to 1907 CE; late 5667 converts to 1908 CE.

13   Genesis 1:1–5 and Genesis 1:14–19.

14   Genesis 1:9–13 and Genesis 1:24–31.

15   Isaiah 45:12

16   (i) Although the analysis in the book proceeds, from first principles, to derive that there are five critical periods of which four have already occurred; the sources (see (ii) and (iii) below) ascertain the same.

(ii) Yitzchak Ginsburgh, *The Hebrew Letters—Channels of Creative Consciousness*, (Jerusalem: Gal Einai Publications, 1990), p. 91.

> The Hebrew alphabet possesses five final letters [the Hebrew alphabet has 22 letters, of which five have different forms when used at the end of a word]. They allude to five ends, or redemptions from the darkness of our exile within the consciousness of plurality to the light of the final awareness of God's absolute unity. We are taught that the first four ends . . . have already become (partially) manifest in the redemptions of the past. The final end awaits the coming of the Mashiach.

(iii) Michael Friedlander, *Pirkê de Rabbi Eliezer* (Illinois: Varda Books, 2004), pp. 382-383.

> *Rabbi Ishmael said : The five fingers of the right hand of the Holy One, blessed be He, all of them appertain to the mystery of the Redemption.*
>
> *Rabbi Eliezer said : The five letters of the Torah, which alone of all the letters in the Torah are of double (shape), all appertain to the mystery of the Redemption.*

CHAPTER 5

1   Genesis Midrash Rabbah 38:13.

2   Genesis 27:18 to Exodus 1:8.

3   Genesis 41:25–32. During the seven years of plenty, Joseph oversaw the amassing of great quantities of grain. In the ensuing years of famine, when everyone (including those outside of Egypt) ran out of food, Joseph still had plenty of grain.

4   "Scripture never states explicitly that the tribe of Levi was not enslaved. In Midrash Tanchuma (Va'erah 6), however, Rabbi Joshua ben Levi makes this assertion. Rashi (on Exodus 5:4) sees it as implicit from the fact that Aaron was able to go and greet Moses, and they were both allowed to come and go as they please—and even meet Pharaoh. How would they be roaming so freely if their tribe was bound in labor? Rather, since the tribe of Levi was a priestly class, even in Egypt, the Egyptians allowed them complete freedom." Menachem Posner, "Why didn't Pharaoh enslave the tribe of Levi?", Chabad–Lubavitch Media Center 1993–2014, http://www.chabad.org/library/article_cdo/aid/811168/jewish /Why-didnt-Pharaoh-enslave-the-tribe-of-Levi.htm

5   Exodus 1:22.

6   Exodus 1:8-10.

7   Exodus 3:3 to 34:35.

8   Exodus 17:8–15. Moses is not commanded to destroy Amalek as the final redemption is not yet possible.

9   (i) The 10 Commandments were engraved upon two Tablets of Testimony. Exodus 31:18.

(ii) The first Tablets were made by God and inscribed *"by the finger of God"* (Exodus 31:18). When Moses descended the mountain with the first Tablets and saw that the people had committed the sin of the Gold Calf *"he threw down the tablets from his hands and shattered them at the foot of the mountain"* (Exodus 32:19). The second Tablets, given after the sin of the Golden Calf, were of a lower level; the script was God's but the stones were carved by Moses (Exodus 34:1). The first Tablets were not totally lost, as Moses was instructed to place their broken fragments into the Holy Ark along with the second Tablets (Babylonian Talmud Bava Basra 14b.)

10   *"They shall make a Sanctuary for me* [God] *so that I may dwell among them."* (Exodus 25:8).

11   I and II Samuel and I and II Kings.

12   After Samson's death in 2831, the Philistines remained subdued until they were sure Samson had no descendants. Then there was period of conquest climaxing in 2870 with the Philistines capturing the Holy Ark and the Tabernacle being destroyed. The Holy Ark was later returned, eventually brought to Jerusalem by King David and placed in the First Temple after Solomon built the Holy Temple in Jerusalem. Just prior to the destruction of the First Temple the Holy Ark was buried or hidden.

13   The books of Ezra and Nehemiah, and Esther.

14   (i) Ezra, also called Ezra the Scribe, and Ezra the high priest in the book of Ezra. In 3413 (348 BCE) Ezra returned to Israel from the Babylonian exile and reinforced Torah law; he also named Jewish months of the Hebrew calendar based on Babylonian month names—that stand to this day.

(ii) Babylonian Talmud Sanhedrin 21b *"Ezra was worthy of the Torah to have been given to Israel though him, had Moses not preceded him."*

15 Esther was a Jewish queen of the Persian king Ahasuerus. Her story is told in the biblical Book of Esther where the Jews are saved from extermination by a descendant of Amalek.

16 A minister in the Persian King Artaxerxes' court, he returned to Israel in 3426 (335 BCE) to strengthen the fledgling Jewish commonwealth. Under his leadership, the walls surrounding Jerusalem were rebuilt, increasing the city's security against its hostile neighbors. Together with Ezra, he reintroduced the observance of laws of the Torah, many of which had been forgotten in exile. The central figure of the Book of Nehemiah.

17 Mattis Kantor, *The Jewish Time Line Encyclopedia* (New Jersey, Jason Aronson Inc., 1992), pp. 99–108.

18 The Maccabees was the name of the Jewish army that revolted against the Syrian-Greek occupation in 139 BCE, whose miraculous victory culminated in the festival of Chanukah. Their name is an acronym of their battle cry, whose Hebrew words mean "who is likened unto You amongst all powers, O, God."

19 Bar Kokhba's original name was Simeon ben Kosiba. He died in battle when the rebellion against Rome was defeated. For a period of time, Rabbi Akiba believed that perhaps he was the Messiah. Rabbi Akiba was a leading contributor to the Mishna and is referred to in the Talmud as Head of all the Sages. See "Bar Kokhba and Bar Kokhba War," *Jewish Encyclopedia*, 2002-2011, http://jewishencyclopedia.com/articles/2471-bar-kokba-and-bar-kokba-war#anchor2.

20 Rabbi Yehudah HaNasi was the editor of the Mishna in its final form. He is referred to as "Rebbi," Teacher par excellence, and

as "Rabbeinu HaKadosh," our Holy Rabbi. He was the son of Rabbi Shimon ben Gamliel II, and was born 80 years after the destruction of the Second Temple. He was a key leader of the Jewish community of Judea toward the end of the 2nd century CE, during the occupation by the Roman Empire. He is best known as the chief redactor and editor of the Mishna. God gave both the Written Law and the Oral Law to Moses on Mount Sinai. The Oral Law was relayed by God to Moses and from him, transmitted and taught to the sages of each subsequent generation Fearing that Oral Law might be lost, Judah HaNasi undertook the mission of committing it to writing in the form of the Mishna.

[21] (i) For the events leading to Joseph's release from prison see Genesis 40:5–23. In Genesis 40:20 Joseph asks the chamberlains to put in a good word for him with the pharaoh, rather than relying on God. This mistake leads to a two-year delay in his release: see Genesis 41:1.

(ii) *The Stone Edition Chumash, the Torah, Haftaros, and Five Megillos, with a Commentary from Rabbinic Writings*, General Editors Rabbi Nosson Scherman and Rabbi Meir Zlotowitz (New York: Mesorah Publications Ltd., 2009), p. 220.

[22] Ibid.

[23] We do not have a birth date for Ezra, only a death date and other dates related to his activities. The birth date is inferred from the overall pattern of history and the death date.

[24] Ibid. for Bar Kokhba.

[25] Exodus 17:8–15. Moses is not commanded to destroy Amalek as the final redemption is not yet possible. Note that this battle with Amalek occurs later in the pattern than the battles in subsequent critical periods.

26   Babylonian Talmud Sanhedrin 93b.

1   (i) Mattis Kantor, *The Jewish Time Line Encyclopedia* (New Jersey, Jason Aronson Inc., 1992), pp 105–107.

(ii) Rabbi Moshe ben Maimon (Rambam), *Mishneh Torah, The Book of Judges, The Laws of Kings and their Wars*, translated by Eliyahu Touger, (Jerusalem: Moznaim publishers, 2001), Chapter 11 Section 4.

2   The significance of Bar Kokhba can be understood by the fact that the battle that ended his life took place on Tish'a B'Av. Tish'a B'Av is regarded as the saddest day in the Jewish calendar and a day destined for tragedy. It is an annual fast day in Judaism, which commemorates tragic events including the destruction of the First and Second Temples in Jerusalem. Rabbi Shmuel Yerushalmi, *The Torah Anthology, The Book of Eicha - Me'am Lo'ez* (New York: Moznaim Publishing Corporation, 1990), segment 4(a)-(e), pp. 2-3.

3   (i) *The Stone Edition Chumash, the Torah, Haftaros, and Five Megillos, with a Commentary from Rabbinic Writings*, General Editors Rabbi Nosson Scherman and Rabbi Meir Zlotowitz (New York: Mesorah Publications Ltd., 2009), p. 145.

> The Four Kingdoms: Jacob [in his dream—Genesis 28:12] was shown the guardian angels of the Four Kingdoms that would ascend to dominate Israel. Jacob saw each angel climbing a number of rungs corresponding to the years of its dominion, and then descending, as its reign ended: [the first kingdom] Babylon's angel climbed seventy rungs and then went down; [the second kingdom] Media's angel [climbed] fifty–two [rungs]; [the third kingdom] Greece's [angel climbed] 130 [rungs]—but the angel of Edom/Esau [the fourth kingdom] kept climbing indefinitely, symbolizing the current exile [initiated by Rome], which seems to be endless.

Jacob was frightened, until God assured him that he would receive Divine protection and eventually return to the Land.

(ii) Each of the four exiles is qualitatively different, as follows: the 1st exile—the Babylonian exile was emotional, demanding the people submit to the king and his idolatry; the 2nd exile—the exile while living under Persian (Median) domination was bodily, as people were threatened with annihilation through the genocidal machinations of Haman; the 3rd exile—the exile while living under Greek cultural domination was intellectual, as the people were subject to harsh decrees prohibiting their religious practice; and, the 4th exile—the current exile (Roman) is combination of emotional, bodily and intellectual, as it has included aspects of all the other exiles: expulsion, mass murder, and persecution. "Mikeitz (Genesis 4:11-44:17) Exile and Return (Part 2)," www.aish.com/tp/b/sw/48955446.html

CHAPTER 6

1   Genesis 27:18–28:5 and Genesis 32:4–33:15.

2   Ezekiel 38 and 39.

3   Genesis 25:22–24.

4   Genesis 27:18–28:5.

5   Genesis 28:10: Jacob goes on his personal exile to escape Esau, spends 14 years studying with Eber and Shem, then 20 years with Laban where he works, marries his wives, and has all but one of his children before leaving. Then he spends two years traveling back home.

6   Genesis 32:4–33:15.

7   "Wiping Out Amalek," 2014, Aish.com,
    http://www.aish.com/atr/Wiping_Out_Amalek.html

8   Ashkenazi Jews are a Jewish ethnic division whose ethno genesis
    and emergence as a distinct community of Jews traces back to
    immigrants originating in the Israelite tribes of the Middle East
    who coalesced in the Roman Empire around the year 1000 CE.
    They established communities throughout Central and Eastern
    Europe, which had been their primary region of concentration
    and residence until recent times, evolving their distinctive
    characteristics and diasporic identity. Their residence in Europe
    was largely brought to an end following the Holocaust. Most
    Jews in America today are Ashkenazic.

9   (i) "Wiping Out Amalek," 2014, Aish.com,
    http://www.aish.com/atr/Wiping_Out_Amalek.html

    (ii) Babylonian Talmud Megillah 6b identifies a nation called
    "Germamia" as the descendants of Amalek. Although some
    interpret this as Germany the original reference is believed to be
    to Cimmerians, which are usually linguistically regarded as
    Iranian. Both interpretations may be correct.

10 Genesis 35:22–26.

11 Genesis 46:1–6.

12 Genesis 50:12-13.

13 Babylonian Talmud Sotah 13a.

    *...because the sons of Esau, of Ishmael and of Keturah also came. A
    Tanna taught: They all came to wage war [against the Israelites]; but
    when they saw Joseph's crown hanging upon Jacob's coffin, they all took
    their crowns and hung them upon his coffin.*

14 "*He* [one of Jacob's grandsons] *took a club and struck [Esau] on the head so that his eyes fell out and rolled to the feet of Jacob.*" Babylonian Talmud Sotah 13a, other sources indicate Esau was killed by one of Jacob's sons.

15 Zohar Vayera, 203.

16 Although slavery begins at this point, the seeds of slavery are visible at the time of Jacob's death. The Egyptians refuse to let the young children go out of Egypt with the rest of the family members to bury Jacob. Thus, although at that time Jacobs descendants were "free" they were not free to leave Egypt. Similarly, for us today, the seed of whatever awaits us at the beginning of the Messianic era is already visible.

17 Rabbi Jacob Immanuel Schochet, *Mashiach: The Principle of Mashiach and the Messianic Era in Jewish Law and Tradition, Expanded Edition,* (USA: Sichos in English, 1988–2009). Appendix II, Mashiach Ben Yossef,
    http://www.sichos-in-english.org/books/mashiach/11.htm

18 Rashi on Genesis 47:28.

19 Babylonian Talmud Sotah 11b.

    And the Egyptians made the children of Israel to serve with rigour. R. Eleazar said: "[It means] with a tender mouth" which the commentary explains "that they induced the Israelites to work by using smooth words to them."

20 Genesis 50:25.

21 (i) Rashi on Exodus 13:19.

    (ii) Ramban on Genesis 49:31.

22 Leviticus 18:1-5.

The Lord spoke to Moses saying, Speak to the Children of Israel and say to them: I am the Lord your God. Do not perform the practice of the land of Egypt in which you dwelled; and do not perform the practice of the land of Canaan to which I bring you, and do not follow their traditions. Carry out My laws and safeguard My decrees to follow them; I am the Lord your God. You shall observe My decrees and My laws which man shall carry out and by which he shall live. I am the Lord.

23   Jerusalem Talmud Berachos 1:5.

24   Rabbi Meir Zlotowitz, Bereishis, *Genesis / a new translation with a commentary anthologized from Talmudic Midrashic and Rabbinic sources* (NY: Mesorah Publications Ltd., 1977), "The Exile Closes in," p. 2074.

25   "Jacob's descent to Egypt alludes to the present exile." Ramban on Genesis 47:28.

26   Genesis 36:1.

27   Genesis 16:1-4.

28   Genesis 16:12.

29   Rabbi Meir Zlotowitz, *Bereishis, Genesis/A New Translation with a Commentary Anthologized from Talmudic Midrashic and Rabbinic Sources* (New York: Mesorah Publications, Ltd., 1977), pp. 551-552 on Genesis 16:12.

30   Genesis 16:6.

31   Ramban on Genesis 16:6.

32   Rashi on Genesis 21:9-10.

33   Genesis 17:18-19.

34 Genesis 21:9-13.

35 Genesis 21:15.

36 Genesis 21:18.

37 (i) Book of Jubilees 20:13-14.

> *And Ishmael and his sons, and the sons of Keturah and their sons, went together and dwelt from Paran to the entering in of Babylon in all the land which is towards the East facing the desert. And these mingled with each other, and their name was called Arabs, and Ishmaelites.*

(ii) Eph'al, I., ""Ishmael" and "Arab(s)": A Transforma-tion of Ethnological Terms," *Journal of Near Eastern Studies* 35 (4), October, 1976, pp. 225–235. doi:10.1086/372504

38 *"These were the years of Ishmael's life...and he expired..."* Expired is not used in scripture except regarding the righteous. Rashi on Genesis 25:17.

39 Genesis 26:34-35.

40 *"So he [Esau] went to Ishmael and married Mahalath, the sister of Nebaioth and daughter of Ishmael son of Abraham, in addition to the wives he already had"* (Genesis 28:9).

41 Ezekiel 38:1-7.

42 Rabbi Moshe Eisemann, *The Book of Ezekiel Vol. 2 / a new translation with a commentary anthologized from Talmudic, Midrashic, and Rabbinic sources* (NY: Mesorah Publications Ltd., 1980), pp. 582-584.

43 Genesis Midrash Rabbah 67:8 and Midrash Tehillim

44 Daniel 2:31-45.

45 We discussed these four kingdoms in Chapter 2, note 35. See also Rabbi Hersh Goldwurm, *Daniel / a new translation with a commentary anthologized from Talmudic, Midrashic, and Rabbinic sources, Seventh Impression* (NY: Mesorah Publications Ltd., 2006), commentaries on Daniel 2:37-40, pp. 102-104.

46 Ibid. commentaries on Daniel 2:41-44, pp. 106-107. Note that one of these commentaries was written in the early 1000s and the other in the early 1800s.

47 Ibid. p. 109. Note that this commentary was written in the early 1000s.

48 Rabbi Moshe Eisemann, *The Book of Ezekiel Vol. 2 / a new translation with a commentary anthologized from Talmudic, Midrashic, and Rabbinic sources* (NY: Mesorah Publications Ltd., 1980), pp. 592-593.

49 Babylonian Talmud Shabbos 118a.

50 Kol HaTor 2:131. *The Voice of the Turtledove*, written by Rabbi Hillel Rivlin of Shklov, a disciple of the Vilna Gaon.

51 Zohar Shemot 32a.
http://www.breslev.co.il/articles/spirituality_and_faith/kabbalah_and_mysticism/edom_and_yishmael.aspx?id=14335&language=english

52 Zohar Vayera 1:119a.

53 Rabbi Moshe Eisemann, *The Book of Ezekiel Vol. 2 / a new translation with a commentary anthologized from Talmudic, Midrashic, and Rabbinic sources* (NY: Mesorah Publications Ltd., 1980), pp. 584, note on *v.* 8.

54 *"And Abraham again took a wife, and her name was Keturah"* Genesis 25:1. *"Keturah is Hagar. Why is she called Keturah? For her deeds were*

[now] as pleasing as the ketoret." Midrash Rabbah on Genesis 25:1. The offering of the ketoret was the most prestigious and sacred of the services in the Holy Temple. The ketoret was a special blend of eleven herbs and balms whose precise ingredients and manner of preparation were commanded by God to Moses.

55   There is much discussion about what these gifts were. Mystical tradition says the following (Zohar Vayera 80-89):

> *Rabbi Abba said: I once was in a town where the children of the east live, and they taught me some of their ancient wisdom and showed me their books of wisdom.... I said to them, my children, all of this is similar to what we have in our Torah, but you should avoid these books, to avoid idolatry.... The ancient children of the east possessed a wisdom which they had inherited from Abraham, who had imparted it to the children of his other wife... in time they followed that wisdom to many false roads.*

56   Genesis 25:5-6. Note that Ishmael is also a concubine child. However, Ishmael participated in Abraham's burial (Genesis 25:9) therefore he could not have been sent away, like Keturah's children.

57   Genesis Rabbah 61:7

58   Akiva Tatz, "End of Days–End of Days", audio lecture, http://www.simpletoremember.com/authors/a/rabbi-akiva-tatz/

59   Ezekiel 38:16.

60   Vital statistics: Jewish population of the World 2014, http://www.jewishvirtuallibrary.org/jsource/Judaism/jewpop.html

CHAPTER 7

[1]   (i) Pesachim 54b; Midrash Tehilim 9:2.

(ii) J. Immanuel Schochet, "Moshiach 101, Date of Mashiach's Coming," Chabad–Lubavitch Media Center, 1993–2014, http://www.chabad.org/library/moshiach/article_cdo/aid/101 680/jewish/Date-of-Mashiachs-Coming.htm

[2]   Sanhedrin 98a.

[3]   Isaiah 60:22.

[4]   J. Immanuel Schochet, "Hastening the Coming of Mashiach", Chabad.org, 2014, http://www.chabad.org/library/moshiach/article_cdo/aid/101 681/jewish/Hastening-Mashiach.htm

[5]   (i) *"Be holy because I, the Lord your God, am holy."* Leviticus 19:12.

(ii) *"Be holy,* i.e., conduct yourselves with thoughtful reservation, making certain that all [your] deeds are for the sake of Heaven." Eli Touger, "What Does Being Holy Mean?" Adapted from *Likkutei Sichos*, Vol. I, p. 254ff; Vol. XII, p. 91ff, Chabad–Lubavitch Media Center, 1993–2014, http://www.chabad.org/library/article_cdo/aid/82715/jewish/ In-the-Garden-of-the-Torah-Kedoshim.htm

[6]   Deuteronomy 30:2-3.

[7]   The Stone Edition Chumash, the Torah, Haftaros, and Five Megillos, with a Commentary from Rabbinic Writings, General Editors Rabbi Nosson Scherman and Rabbi Meir Zlotowitz (New York: Mesorah Publications Ltd., 2009), p. 491. Rabbi Bachya explains that:

> *the Sabbath is the principle of faith and it is equivalent to all of the commandments, for through the commandment of the Sabbath one*

expresses his belief in the creation of the world, that it was created in six days, and that He rested on the seventh. The Sages expound that Jerusalem was destroyed only because they desecrated the Sabbath . . . and that if Israel would but observe two Sabbaths, they would be redeemed immediately.

8   Babylonian Talmud Shabbath 118b.

9   *"Charity is equivalent to all the other religious precepts combined"* Babylonian Talmud Baba Bathra 9a.

10   Isaiah 56:1.

11   Maimonides, *The Laws of Repentance*, 3:4.

CHAPTER 8

1   Rabbi Jacob Immanuel Schochet, *Mashiach: The Principle of Mashiach and the Messianic Era in Jewish Law and Tradition, Expanded Edition,* (USA: Sichos in English, 1988–2009). Appendix II Mashiach Ben Yossef,
http://www.sichos-in-english.org/books/mashiach/11.htm

2   In the tradition handed down by the sages, *"He is the first redeemer, he is the last redeemer"* refers to the Messiah, the last redeemer being the reappearance of the soul of Moses, the first redeemer. Yitzchak Ginsburgh, "Mashiach and Jewish Leadership: Part 12—Moses and Mashiach: Selflessness and Compassion", Gal Einai Publication Society, 1996–2011,
http://www.inner.org/leader/leader12.htm

3   One of the promises of the Messianic Era pertains to the level of revelation: *"A new Torah will emit from Me"* (Midrash Rabbah Leviticus based on Isaiah 51:4). In fact, *"The Torah which man learns in this world is vanity in comparison to the Torah* [which will be

learnt in the days] *of the Messiah*" (Midrash Rabbah, Ecclesiastes XI, 8).

[4] The Ba'al Shem Tov was born in 5458 (1698 CE) and died in 5520. During his life he founded the movement of Chasidim (his joyous expression of Judaism based on the kabbalah of the Arizal) and attracted thousands of followers (many in secret). He began teaching the concepts of Chasidut publicly in 5496. All new revelations begin at the beginning of the 500-year period— e.g., Abraham in the first period smashing idols (year 2000), and in this last period the Ba'al Shem Tov beginning the revelation of the inner Torah (approx. 5500).

[5] (i) Epistle of the Ba'al Shem Tov (Letter to Rabbi Avraham Gershon Kitover):

> *On Rosh Hashana [Jewish new year] of the year 5507, I [Ba'al Shem Tov] made an oath and elevated my soul in the manner known to you . . . the things which I saw and learned when I ascended there would be impossible to communicate . . . I went up from level to level until I entered the palace of the Massiah . . . I asked the Massiah, "when will you come, Master?" and he replied, "by this shall you know: it will be a time when your teachings [of the inner and mystical Torah] become publicized and revealed to the world . . . ."*

(ii) Yitzchak Ginsburgh, "The Death of Moses, the Birth of Mashiach," Gal Einai Publication Society, 1996–2011, http://www.inner.org/audio/aid/E_037.php

[6] Naftali Silberberg, "Moshiach 101: The Resurrection Process," Chabad.org, 2014, http://www.chabad.org/library/moshiach/article_cdo/aid/112 7503/jewish/The-Resurrection-Process.htm

> *The order of the Messianic redemption is as follows: First, Moshiach comes and rebuilds the Holy Temple in Jerusalem. The ingathering of*

all the exiles will then follow. The resurrection of the dead will occur forty years after the exiles return to the Land of Israel. Tzaddikim, the saintly righteous men and women of the generations, are an exception to this rule; they will be resurrected immediately with the arrival of Moshiach.

[7]   See Rabbi David Sedley (edited by the Morasha Curriculum Team), "The World to Come: Part I," NLE Resources, Jerusalem.   http://nleresources.com/nle-morasha-syllabus/spirituality-and-kabbalah/the-world-to-come-iii-the-new-you-resurrection-of-the-dead/

[8]   *"The resurrection of the dead will occur forty years after the exiles return to the Land of Israel."* Naftali Silberberg, "Moshiach 101: The Resurrection Process," Chabad.org, 2014, http://www.chabad.org/library/moshiach/article_cdo/aid/112 7503/jewish/The-Resurrection-Process.htm

[9]   Rabbi Aryeh Kaplan, *Sefer Yetzirah, The Book of Creation: revised edition* (San Francisco; Weiser Books, 1997), 1:7, p. 57.

[10]   Babylonian Talmud, Sanhedrin 38b.

[11]   Yitzchak Ginsburgh, *The Mystery of Marriage* (Israel: Gal Einai Publication Society, 1999), p. 315.

[12]   (i) Babylonian Talmud, Niddah 17a.

       (ii) Yitzchak Ginsburgh, *The Mystery of Marriage* (Israel: Gal Einai Publication Society, 1999), pp. 394–395.

[13]   Exodus Midrash Rabbah 32:1.

[14]   "Amalek (the grandson of Esau), personifies the primordial snake of the Garden of Eden." Rabbi Yitzchak Ginsburgh, "Kabbalah and Medicine, The Healing of Body and Soul, Part

35, The Snake", Gal Einai Publication Society, 1996–2011, http://www.inner.org/healing/healing35.htm

[15] *"the day you eat of it* [the fruit], *you shall surely die."* Genesis 2:17; explanation in *The Essential Malbim* (New York: Mesorah Publications Ltd., 2009), pp. 52-61.

[16] Yitzchak Ginsburgh, *The Hebrew Letters—Channels of Creative Consciousness*, (Jerusalem: Gal Einai Publications, 1990), p. 91.

[17] Rabbi Aryeh Kaplan, *Sefer Yetzirah, The Book of Creation: revised edition* (San Francisco; Weiser Books, 1997), p. 105.

[18] Rabbi Aryeh Kaplan, *Sefer Yetzirah, The Book of Creation: revised edition* (San Francisco; Weiser Books, 1997), p. 105.

[19] Yitzchak Ginsburgh, *The Hebrew Letters—Channels of Creative Consciousness*, (Jerusalem: Gal Einai Publications, 1990), pp. 193,207,265,251,167.

[20] The leader of the generation, Mordechai, who was Esther's cousin, was "in his generation equivalent to Moses in his generation" (Esther Rabbah 6:2) and "was the shepherd of the faith for all the members of his generation (Rabbi Menachem M. Schneerson, "Ve'atah Tetzaveh, Part VII," http://www.chabad.org/library/article_cdo/aid/145422/jewish /Veatah-Tetzaveh-Part-VII.htm).

CHAPTER 9

[1] Zohar Vayera 119a, Ramban on Genesis 2:3 maintains that the seven days of creation correspond to seven millennia of the existence of natural creation. The tradition teaches that the seventh day of the week, Shabbat or the day of rest, corresponds to the

Great Shabbat, the seventh millennium (years 6000–7000), the age of universal rest.

2   Based on the teachings of the Lubavitcher Rebbe, Rabbi Menachem Mendel Schneerson; adapted by Yanki Tauber, "The Resurrection of the Dead," Chabad.org http://www.chabad.org/library/moshiach/article_cdo/aid/262 6/jewish/The-Resurrection-of-the-Dead.htm

3   Ibid.

4   Babylonian Talmud Berachot 34b.

5   Exodus Midrash Rabbah 32:1.

6   Rabbi Isaac Luria teaches that the word Adam is an acronym for Adam, David and Messiah. Had Adam and Eve not sinned, Adam would have retained his true identity, Eve would have manifested the level of King David and their son would have been the Messiah (and would have been born on Day 7). Yitzchak Ginsburgh, *The Mystery of Marriage* (Israel: Gal Einai Publication Society, 1999), p. 356, note 124.

7   Genesis 3:23-24.

8   Yitzchak Ginsburgh, "The Clarification of Evil, The Inner Meaning of *Tu B'Av*" (Gal Einai Publication Society, 1996–2011), www.inner.org/audio/aid/L_901.htm

9   *"the day you eat of it, you shall surely die."* Genesis 2:17.

10   (i) "*and the dust returns to the earth as it was, and the spirit returns to God, Who gave it.*" Ecclesiastes 12:7.

(ii) The World of the Souls is also referred to as The Garden of Eden. Post Adam's sin the Garden of Eden stopped existing on Earth but continued to exist in the spiritual world.

11 Throughout time a particular soul can be reincarnated into another body. However, only those parts of the soul that were not rectified in the earlier incarnation reincarnate in the new body: in order to have the opportunity to be rectified. The part of the soul that had already been rectified in the earlier incarnation remains in the World of the Souls and awaits the time of the resurrection of the dead. This process of reincarnation can occur many times. At the End of Days, "at the time of resurrection of the dead, only those parts [of the soul] that were rectified in the lifetime of that [particular] body return with it" (i.e. each portion of the soul that was rectified in each particular body is resurrected in that body). Rabbi Yitzchak Luria, "Gate of Reincarnations," Chapter Four, Section 3.
http://www.chabad.org/kabbalah/article_cdo/aid/380823/jewish/Reincarnation-and-Resurrection-43.htm

12 The approach of the Ramchal, Rav Tzadok HaKohen, Rav Eliyahu Dessler and Rav Chaim Friedlander found in: Written by Rabbi David Sedley and Edited by the Morasha Curriculum Team, "The World to Come: Part I, II, and III", NLE Resources, Jerusalem.
www.morashasyllabus.com

13 "This World and the Next," (Jerusalem: Ner Le'Elef Booklets, 13 June 2004) p. 39.
http://www.morashasyllabus.com/kabbalah.htm

14 Note that Adam had translucent skin that allowed his soul to be revealed. Only after the sin did he become like us, wherein the soul is concealed by the body:

> *What was the dress of the first man? A skin of nail, and a cloud of glory covered him. When he ate of the fruits of the tree, the nail-skin was stripped off him, and the cloud of glory departed from him, and he saw himself naked . . . .*

Michael Friedlander, *Pirkê de Rabbi Eliezer* (Illinois: Varda Books, 2004), pp. 113-116.

15 More precisely humankind at large will earn eternal life through fulfilling the Noahide commandments (Babylonian Talmud Sanhedrin 105a). Jews start out with the opportunity to receive eternal life in the World to Come (Babylonian Talmud Sanhedrin 11.1). However, the quality of that life is determined by the degree of observance of the commandments and study and connection to Torah. In addition, life in the World to Come can be forfeited via certain actions (Babylonian Talmud Sotah 3b, Ethics of our Fathers 2:8).

16 Written by Rabbi David Sedley and Edited by the Morasha Curriculum Team, "The World to Come: Part III," Section 4, NLE Resources, Jerusalem. www.morashasyllabus.com

17 Lubavitcher Rebbe adapted by Yanki Tauber, *Inside Time—A Chassidic Perspective on the Jewish Calendar* (Meaningful Life Center, 2015), volume 1 p. 87.

18 "This World and the Next," (Jerusalem: Ner Le'Elef Booklets, 13 June 2004) p. 36.
http://www.morashasyllabus.com/kabbalah.htm

19 Based on the teachings of the Lubavitcher Rebbe, Rabbi Menachem Mendel Schneerson; adapted by Yanki Tauber, "The Resurrection of the Dead," Chabad.org
http://www.chabad.org/library/moshiach/article_cdo/aid/262 6/jewish/The-Resurrection-of-the-Dead.htm

20 Rabbi Moshe Chaim Luzzatto, translated by Rabbi Aryeh Kaplan, *Way of G-d: Derech Hashem*, (New York: Feldheim Publishers, 5th edition, November 1, 1981) pp. 47-49.

CHAPTER 10

1   Yitzchak Ginsburgh, "The Clarification of Evil, The Inner Meaning of Tu B'Av", Gal Einai Publication Society, 1996–2011. www.inner.org/audio/aid/L_901.htm

2   Rabbi Mayer Twersky, "Free Will and Divine Providence" The Torah Web Foundation, 1999. http://torahweb.org/torah/1999/parsha/rtwe_vayigash.html

3   Daniel Friedmann, The Broken Gift (USA: Inspired Books, 2013), pp.169-170.

4   See also Rabbi Mayer Twersky, "Free Will and Divine Providence" (The TorahWeb Foundation, 1999). www.torahweb.org/torah/1999/parsha/rtwe_vayigash.html

5   (i) Rav Avraham Brandwein, "Gilgul Neshamot—Reincarnation of Souls," 5756, Jerusalem, Translation by Avraham Sutton. http://vho.org/aaargh/fran/actu/actu00/doc2000/brandwein.html

(ii) Yitzchak Ginsburgh, "The Clarification of Evil, The Inner Meaning of Tu B'Av" (Gal Einai Publication Society, 1996-2011). www.inner.org/audio/aid/L_901.htm.

6   There are exceptions to this under certain circumstances, but the norm is as described.

7   Again, there are exceptions to this under certain circumstances, but the norm is as described.

8   Rambam Hilchot Teshuva 5:1, 3, 4.

APPENDIX A

¹ Mattis Kantor, *The Jewish Time Line Encyclopedia* (New Jersey, Jason Aronson Inc., 1992).

APPENDIX B

¹ (i) Rabbi Yitzchak Ginsburgh "The Ten Sefirot: Introduction," Gal Einai Institute, 5764,
http://www.inner.org/Sefirot/Sefirot.htm

(ii) Nissan Dovid Dubov, "The Sefirot," Chabad–Lubavitch Media Center, 1993–2014,
http://www.chabad.org/library/article_cdo/aid/361885/jewish/The-Sefirot.htm

² Ibid.

³ Drushei Olam HaTohu 2:151b.

> *This is why so much time must transpire from the time of creation until the time of the tikkun [meaning rectification which is due to be completed when the Messiah comes]. All the forces of Gevurot [referring to God absolute power specially to revive the dead] are rooted in the six Sefirot . . . which are the six days of creation . . . and also the 6,000 years of history that the world will exist. And within [the six Sefirot] are the roots of all that will happen from the six days of creation until the Final Tikkun . . . .*

⁴ (i) Ibid.

(ii) Zohar Vayera 119a.

(iii) Sanhedrin 97a.

(iv) Ramban, *Commentary on the Torah,* translated by Rabbi Dr. Charles B. Chavel (NY: Shilo Publishing House, 1971), Genesis, pp. 61–64. This text is reproduced in Appendix C.

[5]   Genesis 1:1-13 and Genesis 1:14-31.

[6]   Genesis 1:1–5 and Genesis 1:14–19.

[7]   Gershom Scholem, *Kabbalah* (NY: Times Books, 1978), p. 111.

[8]   Leviticus 25:3–5.

[9]   Leviticus 25:8–13.

[10]   Yitzchak Ginsburgh, "The Unifications of the Emotive Sefirot", Gal Einai Publication Society, 1996–2011, http://www.inner.org/kabbalah/intermediate/unification-emotive-Sefirot.php

[11]   (i) Although cycles of time in the Torah usually interclude all seven sefirot, and thus form a cycle of seven times seven or 49 periods of time, in the case of human history this is not so. When the cycle is a manifestation of a flow from above to below, as in the case of sabbatical cycles of the land, the 7th sefirah is counted resulting in the usual pattern of seven times seven. However, when the cycle is a manifestation of a flow from below to above, as in the case of the 42 journeys of the Israelites in the dessert (during the 40 years of wandering in the desert, the Israelites encamped 42 times (Numbers 33:1-49)), the 7th sefirah is not counted resulting in a pattern of seven times six or 42. Thus, our journey through history is a pattern of seven times six, that is seven millennia divided into six parts each. When we consider only the six millennia of this world then the pattern is six times six or six millennia each divided into six periods, for a total of 36 periods of time.

Rabbi Yosef Yitzchak Schneersohn, *Creation and Redemption* (NY: Kehot Publication Society, 2007), pp. 76-81.

(ii) Support for the use of a six times six pattern of history can be derived from the fact that the form of the Hebrew letter *lamed* is a composite of the form of three Hebrew letters: *yud, vav* and *kaf* which respectively represent numerical values of 10, 6 and 20 for a total numerical value of 36. And "the letter *lamed* can be seen to represent Jewish history in general, which ever reflects, until a final coming of the Messiah spiraling cycles of hiddenness and revelation, exile and redemption." Why does *lamed* represent Jewish history? Because *lamed* has a numerical value of 30 which represents the month and the cycle of the moon, which are in turn associated with the cycling of history. For example, "the Midrash correlates the 30 days of the month to the 30 generations between Abraham and King Josiah who immediately preceded the destruction of the First Temple. From Abraham until Solomon, the builder of the First Temple, there were 15 generations, corresponding to the 15 days of the waxing of the moon. The generation of Solomon is referred to as the full moon. The waning of the moon begins from Solomon's son, Rechivam, in whose generation the kingdom of Israel was divided and continued for 15 generations to Josiah, one of the greatest tzadikim. . . who was tragically killed in war." Yitzchak Ginsburgh, *The Hebrew Letters—Channels of Creative Consciousness*, (Jerusalem: Gal Einai Publications, 1990), pp. 190-191.

(iii) Further support for the use of a six times six pattern of history can be derived from the fact the world exists in the merit of tzadikim (singular tzadik). A *tzadik* (Hebrew for a consummately righteous person) is someone who is so completely devoted to God that he never regards himself as a separate entity or individual. He is referred to by the phrase "[devoted] *to Him*" which in Hebrew is the word *lamed vav* —

lamed vav has a numerical value of 36. There are also 36 tzadikim in each generation. Yitzchak Ginsburgh, *The Mystery of Marriage* (Israel: Gal Einai Publication Society, 1999), pp. 84-85.

(iv) Further support for the use of a six times six pattern of history can be derived from the fact that in general a tzadik corresponds to the sefirah of foundation, the 6th emotive channel of Divine energy. The full inter–inclusion of six or six times six equals 36 which represent the 36 tzadikim in each generation (Babylonian Talmud Sukah 45b).

(v) Another treatment of years and sefirot is to use all 10 sefirot and form a 10x10 cycle. Using 10 sefirot the first six columns in Table B.4 correspond to the six millennia of history, and the seventh column corresponds to the seventh millennium; the other columns correspond to time not shown in Table B.4. The columns are then inter–included to generate a 10x10 pattern. In this pattern the six millennia of history are therefore subdivided into 10 rows of 100 years, each representing one of the 10 sefirot. Thus, this treatment of history is a 6x10 pattern; unlike our treatment, shown in Table B.4, which divides each millennia of history into six rows of approximately 167 years each (leading to our six times six pattern of history). For an overview of the 6x10 patterns see, for example, Rabbi Yitzchak Ginsburgh, "The Secrets of the Year 5764," Gal Einai Publication Society, September 20, 2003,
http://www.inner.org/audio/aid/L_1019.htm

[12] (i) Yitzchak Ginsburgh, *The Hebrew Letters—Channels of Creative Consciousness*, (Jerusalem: Gal Einai Publications, 1990), p. 105

(ii) There are many other allusions to the importance of 36. For example, during the festival of lights, representing spiritual survival in a physical secular world (effectively the Divine

Purpose), one lights a total of 36 candles: 1 on the first day, 2 on the second day . . . 8 on the eighth day, for a total of 36 candles.

[13] It is interesting to note that 167 is the numerical value of the phrase "*the Lord is our God the Lord is one*"(הוי' אלהינו הוי' אחד) from Deuteronomy 6:4—which verse encapsulates the monotheistic essence of Judaism and is the first verse of the prayer that serves as a centerpiece for both the morning and evening Jewish services.

[14] (i) Although the analysis in the book proceeds, from first principles, to derive that there are five critical periods of which four have already occurred; the sources (see (ii) and (iii) below) ascertain the same. The concept in (ii) and (iii) below is further elaborated in Chapter 8.

(ii) Yitzchak Ginsburgh, *The Hebrew Letters—Channels of Creative Consciousness*, (Jerusalem: Gal Einai Publications, 1990), p. 91.

> *The Hebrew alphabet possesses five final letters [the Hebrew alphabet has 22 letters, of which five have different forms when used at the end of a word]. They allude to five ends, or redemptions from the darkness of our exile within the consciousness of plurality to the light of the final awareness of God's absolute unity. We are taught that the first four ends . . . have already become (partially) manifest in the redemptions of the past. The final end ... [the fifth letter], awaits the coming of the Mashiach.*

(iii) Michael Friedlander, *Pirkê de Rabbi Eliezer* (Illinois: Varda Books, 2004), pp. 382-383.

> *Rabbi Ishmael said: The five fingers of the right hand of the Holy One, blessed be He, all of them appertain to the mystery of the Redemption.*

Rabbi Eliezer said: The five letters of the Torah, which alone of all the letters in the Torah are of double (shape), all appertain to the mystery of the Redemption.

APPENDIX C

[1] Ramban, *Commentary on the Torah*, translated by Rabbi Dr. Charles B. Chavel (NY: Shilo Publishing House, 1971), Genesis, pp. 61–64. Ramban's explanation of the history of the world in terms of the 6 Days of Creation was regarded with approval by many later authors. Bachya ben Asher and Menachem Ricanti copied it verbatim. Surprisingly it found its way into Egypt, and was wholly incorporated into the Midrash Rabbi David Hanagid, (Book of Exodus, pp. 201–2, ed. by A. Katz), the grandson of Maimonides.

Index

175

Land of Israel   25, 26, 27, 28, 36, 64, 72, 118, 119, 123
Levi   45, 54, 58, 59, 120

Maccabees   48, 120
Magog   26, 55, 60, 63, 64, 65, 70, 71, 75, 76, 118
Maze   1, 2, 3, 4, 24, 25, 30, 90, 120
Messiah   3, 24, 25, 26, 27, 29, 30, 52, 59, 64, 66, 67, 68, 70, 71, 72, 75, 76, 78, 81, 82, 83, 87, 114, 120, 121, 126, 135
Messiah ben David   29, 30, 59, 120, 121
Messiah ben Joseph   29, 59, 60, 71, 121
Messianic Era   3, 7, 11, 16, 17, 23, 26, 29, 63, 67, 71, 79, 81, 87, 118, 121, 122, 124
Middle East   57, 65
Midrash   121
 Midrashim   121, 122
 Rabbah   121
millennia of history   33, 101
Millennium   7, 17, 35, 36, 37, 38, 39, 40, 41, 43, 73, 74, 75, 77, 81, 101, 104, 105, 107, 111, 124
Mishna   48, 51, 52, 70, 78, 79, 114, 121
Moses   4, 5, 7, 16, 17, 20, 21, 36, 45, 46, 50, 51, 52, 56, 70, 71, 95, 103, 104, 117, 118, 120, 121, 124, 125, 126
Mount Sinai   15, 16, 46, 95, 121

Nebuchadnezzar   47, 63
Nehemiah   9, 48, 118, 121, 125, 127
Noah   34, 36, 109, 122
Noahide Laws   14, 15, 16, 27, 67, 85, 122
non-Abrahamic   1, 62, 117

Oral Law   5, 122, 126

Patriarchs   27, 62, 103, 106, 113, 119
Pattern   36, 37, 40, 50, 51, 71, 99
peace   2, 3, 21, 26, 28, 29, 54, 55, 57, 58, 67, 68, 76, 81, 82, 86, 87, 121, 125, 135
people of the Far East   65
period
 critical   11, 20, 35, 38, 39, 40, 41, 43, 44, 45, 46, 47, 48, 49, 50, 51, 53, 54, 58, 59, 69, 70, 71, 72, 73, 74, 77, 78, 79, 83, 105, 106, 107, 108, 115, 116, 117, 122
 preparatory   41, 44, 45, 50, 52, 53, 58, 64, 73, 74, 106, 107
Persia   48, 63
Persian   8, 22, 116, 117, 121
Philistines   46, 47, 123, 124
Promised Land   45, 46, 113, 121
prophecies   23, 25, 29, 30, 52, 53, 58, 60, 64, 68, 69, 82, 95, 116, 119
Prophets   116, 126
Psalms   5, 64, 116, 127

www.ingramcontent.com/pod-product-compliance
Lightning Source LLC
LaVergne TN
LVHW051630080426
835511LV00016B/2277